american prom

american
PROM

RICHARD G. CALO, PH.D.

Cumberland House
Nashville, Tennessee

American Prom
Published by Cumberland House Publishing
431 Harding Industrial Drive
Nashville, TN 37211

Cover design: Karen Phillips
Text design: Julie Pitkin

Library of Congress Cataloging-in-Publication Data

Calo, Richard G., 1964-
    American prom / Richard G. Calo.
        p. cm.
    ISBN-13: 978-1-68162-930-8 (pbk. : alk. paper)
    ISBN-10: 1-68162-930-5 (pbk. : alk. paper)
    1. Proms.   2. Proms--Social aspects--United States.   3. Proms
--Social aspects--Canada.   I. Title.
GV1746.C25 2006
394'.3--dc22

                                                    2006020625

Printed in the United States
1 2 3 4 5 6 7 — 12 11 10 09 08 07 06

For Sebastian, Christian, and Julian

One day you, too, will go to your proms.

We'll talk then...

Contents

Acknowledgments

This book was made possible through the more than twenty thousand submissions to www.ThePromSite.Com from visitors who took the time out to leave me with their story or thoughts about prom night. My thanks go to them. Also, a special acknowledgment to those contributors whose material I selected for printing here. It is wonderful stuff and has given us all a deeper and broader insight into the magic of prom and into the hearts and minds of teens in the United States and Canada. Thanks also go to everyone I interviewed. Their patience helped me get this prom thing in perspective.

A special thanks to my wife, Dr. Clara Somoza, who read through the evolving manuscript and kindly explained why I shouldn't use some of those big words.

american prom

Wait! Stop!

Have you got a prom story?
Do you remember your prom as a wonderful time?
Something so special that you have to tell us about it?
Have you got some thoughts on prom
and would like to share them?

Because we would certainly love to hear them—all of us:
me, people who are going to prom,
people who have been to prom,
people who haven't been but would like to know more about it.
Everyone.

So please take a few moments to visit

www.*The*PromSite.Com

and submit your stories and thoughts.

We look forward to hearing from you!

Introduction

How Could I Have Forgotten?

Did you ever wonder what prom-goers do prom night, what they think and how they feel?

Not me.

My own prom safely over, I somehow forgot the importance it once held for me, the feelings it evoked, the sense of expectation, the hours I spent imagining what it would be like on *that* night, dancing with my high school love. Would I finally work up the nerve to kiss her? Would we start going out, or, as they say these days, hook up? Would I be able to show my friends that I finally had a real girlfriend, about whom I was deadly serious? I recall that these were paramount issues for me at the time, more important than passing my classes or absorbing what the teachers had to offer.

Then prom night came and went (yes, I hooked up with her). I graduated and went to college, continued on to a Ph.D. And along the way I forgot, completely forgot, what it had been like for me in those last few months of high school. It was all gone: the expectations, the emotions, everything.

I'd like to say I am the anomaly, that everyone else remembers just fine. But I'm not. Although many of us remember our proms with fondness, same as we do our high school years, we forget the sheer emotional intensity that hovers around the event, the sense of meaning that attaches to it. We won't feel this intensity and meaning again until our wedding day.

It's not just individuals who forget. Our entire adult culture trivializes prom. We consider it a silly teen thing, something to smile indulgently down upon, but not worth sustained attention once we become mature, responsible members of our society. It is no accident, for example, that not a single paper on the phenomenon exists in the anthropological literature. Yet this phenomenon has been with us for a century, and high school students and entire communities devote themselves to it each year to the exclusion of nearly everything else. It is a phenomenon, moreover, that appears to be gathering momentum every year.

What brought the meaning of prom back to me, along with some of its intensity, was not scholarly interest—there's still no academic paper on the phenomenon because I haven't written one, and probably never will. What brought it back was The Calito Dress Company, who asked me in 1999 to create www.PromDress.Net. This was supposed to be a straightforward prom website, with prom fluff here and there, but designed to advertise prom dresses.

It started out that way, too—pictures of dresses, little articles about prom updos, bulleted countdowns, checklists. You know, the whole teeny glamour must-do thing. But then I began collecting "prom stories." They were meant to be more padding for the website. Except that hundreds of stories flooded in, and they were so charged with feeling I had to take notice. I had wanted cutesy stories about glammed up girls. Instead, I got moving stories about true love and the hope and anxiety that come with it. In fact, many of the best stories came from guys, not girls.

I hadn't expected this. Intrigued, I created an advice area so I could interact more directly with prom-goers. That was an instant hit and a healthy percentage of girls started asking about hair and dress and ankle bracelets and who knows what. But a truly robust percentage, guy and girl, started requesting advice on powerful emotional issues. They were more concerned with relationships and sexuality than primping and visuality.

I had to admit something was going on. What was prom? How were teens using it? What were they thinking when they thought prom? What were the feelings associated with it? Why was it so desperately important to them? Lots of questions. None of them about dresses and hair and accessories.

Well, I put on my academic's hat and went to work. I developed questionnaires, I interviewed prom-goers, parents, teachers; I created sections on the website to discuss different aspects of prom. In 2001, I even morphed the original website into www.ThePromSite.Com because it had totally outgrown the prom dress twaddle.

Prom, I had rediscovered, was about a lot more than prom dresses. Certainly it was more than a silly teen thing, and probably it was something deeply meaningful to all of us as a culture.

Graduating and Coming of Age

No, prom is not prom night only. That was lesson number one. Prom has three stages, and you have to combine the three to understand the whole. In this book, I call the stages "Asking," "Prom Night," and "After-Prom." The three are interdependent; they build on each other, sometimes over the space of four or more months, and together form the prom phenomenon, or cultural pattern, or institution, or whatever you want to call it. Like everyone else, I was used to thinking of prom as prom night, one night of party and excess. I had not considered the part before prom night as crushes and boyfriends-girlfriends (bfs-gfs) asking each other to prom and then preparing for the night. Or the part after prom night, when crushes start going out, and bfs-gfs consolidate their relationships, sometimes by admitting genuine love, sometimes by getting engaged.

When viewed like this, prom is not a maximum twenty-four hour experience. The total event happens over many months, from the moment when you decide who to ask to prom, to the moment when you either start going out (crushes), admit love for the first time (bfs-gfs), or party yourself out two or three days after the prom dance (friends).

Why does it require so much time? Because prom is not only about transition. It is also about transformation. Transition is linear; it means you move from one stage to another stage. Transformation is not linear, and it means you stop being one kind of thing and start being another. Prom celebrates the transition from high school into college or the workforce—we all know that. Even junior prom celebrates the transition from mere high school into senior year. We call that graduating, and I'll have more to say about it in a moment. But prom also facilitates—notice I did not say "celebrates"—the less obvious but more important transformation from childhood into responsible young adulthood. And we call *that* coming of age.

Now, the two, *graduating* and *coming of age*, are not the same thing and they are not redundant. Graduating is a legislated event that depends on the institutions a culture creates; and these institutions are not universal. In North America, for example, we create the institution of high school, and then we specifically mark its end with a ceremony, which may or may not include a party. Coming of age, on the other hand, is much more subtle because it *is* universal. It may coincide with an officially declared event like the end of high school, but it doesn't have to. It doesn't have to because it is rooted in human biology (nature), not social structures (culture). Few people outside North America attend a high school, or have a prom. But every human being on the planet comes of age, and this is marked by accession to adult sexuality and its responsibilities (whether we want to accept them or not).

The thing is, in North America, in the US as much as Canada, coming of age happens to have linked up with graduating, in the event we call prom, in what I can only describe as a wonderful historical accident.

Why is prom linked historically with coming of age? Partly, it's tradition (culture). Partly, it's biological mechanics (nature). In terms of tradition, prom arises out of the nineteenth century Victorian "coming out" party, where a girl of the upper classes was presented for the first time to her society as a woman, and there made eligible to those suitors her family had pre-selected for her. As the middle classes (you and me, basically) gained more economic power toward the end of the nineteenth century and into the 20th, we sought to emulate the upper classes' traditions, and prom evolved from imitating the "coming out" party, except we made it egalitarian by opening it up to all individuals, not just the privileged one.

In terms of biological mechanics, prom closely parallels coming of age practices in other parts of the world. These practices are invariably linked with hooking up, or to put it more formally, partner or mate selection. In more traditional societies, as anthropologists sometimes refer to them, the coming of age practices are structured by the authoritative elements of that society, whether parental, clan, or tribal. They are held once a year for the new crop of coming of age youths. They are marked with a party or celebration. And they usually involve the announcement of a betrothal or some kind of formal partnering, or if not an actual partnering, then the recognition that the youth is now of marriageable age. In our society, the coming of age practice is also structured by the authoritative elements of the society, namely, our parents and high schools. The difference between theirs and ours is that we have greater freedom of choice over the partners we choose. Parents, clan, tribe, none of them tell us who we can go out or hook up with, or who we can marry (although parents pretty much always have to approve if you want to keep the peace at home). This wasn't true of upper-class Victorians any more than it is true of European royalty today.

When we took over the Victorian coming out party and evolved it into prom, we jettisoned any taint of institutionally acknowledged now-mature sexuality from the event. We had to, because if we were not going to tell our children who to partner with, we also couldn't tell them when they were of an age to partner—which was the main purpose of the Victorian coming out.

But the need to come of age did not go away just because we excluded it from formal representation in our prom celebration. It has always been there, exerting a subtle influence below the gradua-tion party. And in the last twenty or thirty years, high schoolers have independently and consciously reestablished its original purpose (back when it was the Victorian coming out).

Today, they deliberately use it to mark their coming of age, to each other, and to the world at large, by announcing their first seri-ous boyfriend or girlfriend. They are telling the world that theirs is no longer kid stuff, that something fundamental has changed in their being—they are more adult, more mature. It does not mean they have to have actual sex to prove there has been a change (in fact, that's mis-guided if not stupid, and sure proof they are *not* mature or responsi-ble). The true proof is that they have selected a "real" partner they feel strongly about and about whom, if asked, they would reply "yes, marrying them is a definite possibility."

Consider the following example. Tom has had a crush on Jennifer throughout high school. He does not know if she returns the feelings but he will soon find out because he has decided to ask her to his jun-ior prom. Prom night is mid-May but he asks in February (when the bulk of the asking takes place) because he doesn't want anyone beating him to it. Jennifer says yes and Tom thinks he has a chance or she would have turned him down—so his expectations start to rise. Tom doesn't know this (although he suspects it), but Jennifer has also had a crush on him throughout high school. Yet neither of them has done anything about their feelings, being too young, too inexperienced, or just too shy. Indeed, they have barely spoken over the past four years.

Now they have agreed to go to junior prom together, which means they have entered into a special relationship—we can call it a "pre-relationship," or "testing each other out period." Over the next few months, they will plan for the night and weekend, from transportation to coordinating corsage and boutonniere. This will force them to interact, and they will get to know one another better and start to relax around each other. By the time prom night arrives, they will be pretty certain where they stand and whether or not they will go out. They will even know if their parents and friends agree that they are right for each other.

It will have taken from February to mid-May to get to this point and now comes the evening itself. Tom shows up at her house looking splendid in his tuxedo, and Jennifer looks totally gorgeous as she descends the staircase from her room and Tom sees her for the first time in her gown. Their feelings for each other automatically intensify, and they get so nervous they can barely speak. But...the show must go on and nervous or not, they exchange the coordinated corsage and boutonniere, her parents take pictures, they chat, and slowly the initial stage fright evaporates. They are good to go.

The rest of the evening's stages (think "segments," also think "stage where actors play") are quite literally designed to hook Tom and Jennifer up into a dating couple:

During the first part of prom night—limo, dinner, pics, the dance—it's all elegance and romance as they act out their formal roles. Expectation and feeling builds between Tom and Jennifer as the evening unfolds, and this peaks in the first kiss, especially if this first kiss coincides with the last dance for a perfect denouement.

During the second part of prom night—the school's sponsored after-prom (or private party)—it's all fun and games and party and casual clothes. After-prom gives the couple the time they need to consolidate their brand new relationship. It provides them with a buffer for the climaxed feelings—mostly the release of tension, as well as a gradual wind-down from the heady excitement—that come with having actually hooked up.

By the time they go home next morning, they are formally boyfriend-girlfriend (bf-gf), and the process, which began in February, is now complete.

Two things have happened in terms of this couple's developing maturity. First, by hooking up, they have confirmed to themselves and each other that they are now mature or adult enough to engage in adult practices, with all their attendant seriousness; and second, they have announced this confirmation to the world by appearing in public for the first time as a couple. Suddenly—or so it seems in retrospect—these are no longer kids just playing around. Suddenly, this is a formally dating couple behaving like young adults and requesting to be seen as such. In other words, they have *come of age.* And the institutional vehicle that facilitated this process was prom, from asking through preparation, through the evening itself.

For the sake of calling this process something, I have called it the "crushes-to-couples" process. But I also want to indicate that it is a generalized process; it is not only for crushes. As such, the process works at different levels in different teens depending on where they are in the development (and making public) of their adult sense of sexuality and its responsibilities. What prom does at these different levels is:

It brings crushes together for the first time and transforms them into couples—more new couples are formed on or around prom night, especially junior prom, than the rest of the year put together.

It transforms boyfriend-girlfriend (bf-gf) couples into still tighter units through mutual declarations of love on prom night, or by engagements to be married (or to live together in college, or otherwise cement the current relationship so that it becomes more than "just" bf-gf).

It even facilitates gratuitous sexual encounters among a small percentage of the prom-going population who are not in a relationship but who have been in relationships in the past and whose active (if irresponsible) sexuality is already publicly acknowledged.

Now, before you conclude that prom is always about sexuality and coming of age, or even that I believe it's always about sexuality and coming of age, let me say that no, it is not only about that. That is the coming of age part of it. There's also the graduation part of it. This part is about having fun, which simply means partying with friends, especially if you are going to prom with your best guy or girl friend, toward whom you have no romantic intentions. On average, 35% of prom-goers go with friends, whether as a group or in strictly non-romantic couples, and this is not a last resort tactic after every romantic possibility has been exhausted. They choose to attend prom with friends because it kills the pressure of romance on prom night. It also keeps them from worrying and getting too uptight because they're with their crush and don't want to screw up or look stupid—and pressure, worry, and uptightness translate into not having fun.

Finally, prom is an end of the year event, and for seniors, it is an end of high school event. Two sentiments meet here. One is a sense of ending and "moving on now." The year is over, or high school itself is over; serious, life-altering change is coming. Prom celebrates this ending and change. The second is the feeling that prom night may be the last time all one's friends are together. This also needs celebrating, and can only be celebrated in the presence of those friends.

The crushes-to-couples process runs alongside these sentiments and may not even be present for many of these prom-goers. Which doesn't diminish prom night one bit.

In conclusion, when I now think of prom, I think of two kinds of change: the immediate transition out of high school or into senior year (a graduation), which is a celebration of friendship as much as it is a celebration of endings and new beginnings; and the transformational process that takes place in the last few years of high school, culminating in prom night, and that is all about exercising one's sexuality for the first time (a coming of age), whether by entering into a serious relationship for the first time, or declaring one's love for the first time, or getting engaged (for the first and only time ;-).

How This Book is Arranged

American Prom has five sections, each containing several chapters.

I - Asking.
II - Prom Night.
III - After-Prom.
Together, these three sections outline the prom process, beginning at the moment of asking and ending with the moment when you start going out, or make your declaration of love, or otherwise make your relationship binding (or when the after-prom ends, if there is going to be none of the above).

IV - Embarrassing Moments.
Things go wrong all the time during the prom process—yes, bad things happen even to people in gowns and tuxedos. This section should provide you with plenty of comic relief, because most of the stories are quite funny (at least I thought so). Its goal is to offer a counterpoint to the seriousness and intensity of prom.

V - Traditions.
This last section takes a geographically broad look at how prom night and after-prom are celebrated in North America. I showcase traditions from the United States and Canada to build a picture of the overall evening, and I set out *the master prom script,* an outline of what is common to all or most contemporary proms. The difference between this section and the first three is that the first are all about what teens do for prom, whereas this last is about what schools and communities do.

Glossary.
Some of us older folk might find this useful in understanding current teen or Internet usage. :-)

Who This Book is For

Sure it's for everyone: Everyone who has gone to prom. Everyone who will be going to prom. And everyone else. LOL.

But look, this book really is meant to be *enjoyed*. It is not supposed to be a didactic study of prom, and I prefer to think of it as a snapshot of prom today. It contains 316 stories contributed by people in the US and Canada who have been to prom in the last five years. I include lots of analytic commentary to help us unravel the puzzle that is prom, but I certainly don't want this to eclipse the sheer pleasure I'd like you to get from reading the stories.

In any case, I also hope to accomplish two things:

To present a broad outline of the prom phenomenon and what it means for prom-goers. This is useful for *teens* because it can help you prepare for your own prom. It is useful for *adults* because this book will give you a more sustained glimpse into contemporary prom than has ever been available before. It is useful for *parents* because it can help you understand what teens are preparing for, and how you yourselves should best prepare.

This book also intends **to demonstrate that prom is an important cultural reality for North Americans,** which means we should probably take it more seriously than we (us adults) have in the past, *especially* academic adults like ritualists, sociologists, and anthropologists.

I've had a lot of fun studying prom over the past five years. I had just as much fun writing this book. And now I hope that you will find it *totally off the hook.* Enjoy!

Richard Calo, Ph.D.

ASKING

Introduction

Asking someone to prom is such a big deal that the asker (and the askee) will often agonize for months over the how and the when of it. First, there's the question of who you're going to ask. Always, and I really mean always, the first person you consider asking is the one you've had a crush on "like forever." Then there's the planning stage. You rarely walk up to your crush and say, "Hey, want to go to prom with me?" There's usually some preparation, even if it's only a few flowers, or a lockerful of Hershey's Kisses. Moreover, the preparation itself depends on how well you know the person, not to mention how daring you are. You might be the sort who can jump up on a table in the cafeteria during lunch and ask in front of everybody, knowing this will produce an automatic 'yes'; or you might have a secret crush on the askee and are unsure whether the feelings are returned, so you can't ask in an all-out-romantic way because you might overdo it.

Then there's timing. When do you ask? If you ask too early, the askee may think you're jumping the gun. If you wait too long, someone else might ask him or her before you do. This last can be tricky, and the window of opportunity is quite small: asking takes place up to four months in advance of prom. It starts happening a couple of weeks after New Year's, and steps up during St. Valentine's Day. By the end of February, most of the serious asking—that is, by crushes who are hoping to hook up into couples prom night—has taken place. What's left after this are the second-string hopes and fallback dates when the one you really wanted to go with said no.

Last but not least, there's the stretch of time between asking (and being accepted) and the arrival of prom night. You now need to plan prom night together—who pays for what, what color flower goes on the corsage, how you will get to the dance, etc. This takes some doing; but it also gives the couple more opportunity to be in each other's company. Sometimes, asker and askee hook up during this period, especially if the asker has admitted their feelings in the way they asked, and those feelings are as strongly returned. Most often though (about 70%

of the time), couples wait until prom night, or until the after-prom party, to hook up. In the meantime, they plan the night, and they allow the expectation to build.

In case I just gave you the impression that prom is an expensive and elaborate excuse for turning crushes into couples, let me add that yes, it is that, but not for everyone. Many also go with friends, either in pairs (no hooking up), or as a group. At one junior prom, for example, I estimated that nearly 35% were there with friends. This is completely in sync with the national average: 35% attend with friends, and about 10% of these go in groups, without a date. In any case, none of the prom-goers I spoke to had used elaborate means to ask their partner to attend prom night—there were no flowers, or Build-a-Bears, or wonderfully elaborate preparations. A simple, "Hey, want to go to prom with me?" and they went. The reasons for going with a good friend were always the same. The following words from Cutie22 in Silver Spring, MD, sum it all up:

> IF u like someone romantically then go for it....BUT sometimes it can be even more fun to go with a good friend...then you can dance with other friends...and just not have to worry about what your date is going to do. My best friend is a guy...we went to prom together...it was the best night of my life...we just had so much fun! And it was nice because I knew how he'd react to different things...and I didn't have to worry about the whole sex thing...but I did spend the night at his house...just so we could talk about how much fun we had. So if u have a good guy friend...go 4 it!

Of course, not everyone feels the same as Cutie22 about going with a friend. Some ask their friend to go with them in the last week or two before prom night, and only as a last resort. Why do they wait so long? Because they just spent the last few months trying to get a *romantic* date for prom and it didn't work out. In other words, while some prom-goers may go with a date toward whom they have no romantic intentions, their preference is to go with someone they like.

For those with romantic intentions, however, asking someone to prom is the most important step in the prom process because who you go with determines the outcome of prom night—and how you ask can make all the difference in who you go with. Given its importance, asking has evolved into an often carefully planned and executed event. The 82 stories in this *Asking* section will show you just how intricate it can be. With the exception of the first and last chapter, I have separated the stories into two sets, those in which crushes do the asking and those in which boyfriends and girlfriends (bfs-gfs) do the asking. Bfs-gfs ask each other to prom in ways that are even more involved than the ones crushes use. That they do so, although it's understood they are going together, is ample proof of the importance of being formally asked to prom: asking is not for crushes only. Asking is the step that sets the entire prom process in motion.

(A note on the expression "hook up" and "hooking up": in this book I use it to mean "the moment when a couple *starts* going out, when they first become bf-gf." Most teens use it this way, although you probably won't find this definition in a common usage dictionary. If you think "hook up" means "casual sex," then yes, it means that too, but only when qualified with a well-defined piece of time, such as "hooked up for the night.")

A Play on Words

Some of us use things to play on words when we want to make a point. This also happens to be a very acceptable, enjoyable, often comical way of asking someone formally to prom. It works for crushes, and it works for boyfriends and girlfriends.

Lucy, Battle Ground High School, Battle Ground WA

When I got to my third period class there was a HUGE chunk of ice on my desk. A chisel lay beside it. So I had to chisel my way into the middle of the block, and inside was a note saying, "Now that we've broken the ice, will you go to prom with me?" I was so flattered, and obviously, I said yes!!

Maddi, LCC, Encinitas CA

Okay well I really liked this guy Ryan. I figured he wouldn't want to go with me, but I asked him anyway. The way I did it was I caution-taped his driveway and put WANTED signs with his name on them all over the garage. Then I traced myself on the ground and put ketchup everywhere (as blood). It was a whole crime scene. Then under the traced body I put, "I've been dying to go to prom with you." Then I popped out and asked him myself. Thankfully he said yes! I was sooo Happy!!

Anonymous, Ponderosa High School, Parker CO

Last year I really wanted to go to prom, but I couldn't decide which of these two really hot girls I should ask. I'm a pretty shy guy though, so I kept procrastinating. I finally made up my mind to ask this girl on the tennis team, but prom was rapidly approaching so I had to think of a way to ask her. I try to be a funny guy most of the time, so I tried to think of a way I could include some humor when asking her. I ended

up writing, "Will... You... Go... To... Prom... With... Me?" on tennis balls and then putting them on her car after school. I hid behind
another car out of sight until she read the message. I got out of my
hiding spot and presented her with some flowers and said, "I wanted
to ask you earlier but I had to get the balls to ask you." She appreciat-
ed the humor, gave me a hug and said yes! We had an awesome time,
but I don't recommend prom as the first date—it was long!

Liz, Salt Lake City UT
My boyfriend is really into music. He cut out like over a hundred
musical notes and put them all over my room, and on the back of my
chair he put a piece of paper that said, "Liz, it would be music to my
ears if you would go to prom with me."

Brandon, Brighton High School, Salt Lake City UT
I work with this girl who is soooo beautifully gorgeous. I found her
schedule and went to her house while she was at work. I laid flower
petals from her front door to her bathroom. I laid more petals all
over the bathroom! I filled the tub, put floating candles, three boats,
some sharks, and more flower petals in it. Next to the tub, I placed a
piece of paper that said, "It would float my boat if you would go to
junior prom with me." Rolled up inside one of the boats was another
paper that said, "Look by the toilet." By the toilet, hidden under
flower petals and a towel, was a small bucket of flour. The note on it
said, "Sift through the 'flour' to find my name." But my name wasn't
in there! Instead, I went to her school the next day with a dozen roses
and said, "I gave you the flower." She melted in my arms and started
to cry. Trust me guys, they'll love you for it!

Jessica, Las Vegas High, Las Vegas NV
The guy that asked me filled my bathtub with water and put a bunch of
real goldfish in there and one really pretty colorful fish (I don't even
know what kind it was) and there was a little treasure chest on the bottom with a little poem in it that said, "Of all the fish in the sea, I
chose you to go to prom with me." It was really cute!

Shawn, Tustin High, Tustin CA

I toilet papered her car at school, and put a toilet seat on the hood that said, "If you had to go...would you go with me?" It was great!

Carli, UT

I decorated this boy's room with TONZ of little parachute guys. They were all over his ceiling and walls and bed. Wrapped around each of the little guys was a piece of paper that said things like, "Keep looking." On some of them there were letters to my name. On his wall, I put up a poster. The poster said, "I'd jump at the chance to take you to the dance, so let's get crackin' man to find out who I am, you'll find someone fantastic, when you look under the colored plastic." He had to look through all of the guys to find the letters to my name. The way he answered me was he came to my door and gave me a single rose and a bag of suckers and a note that said, "I'd be a sucker not to go with you."

Leah, MHS

My best friend has always made me laugh so hard that sometimes I cry, but he had never made me feel so special as the day he decided to shut himself in my locker before I got to school. When I got there, I was struggling to get my locker open and it seemed jammed. I finally just kicked it and it fell open. I let out a loud scream as my best friend came tumbling out onto the floor with a sign on his back saying, "I'd die to go to prom with you." I just about wet my pants I was laughing so hard.

Crushes

What's a crush? Basically, anyone whom you've liked for some time
but haven't made a move on. It's no secret that on prom night, most
of those who have a crush on someone would really rather be there
with their crush than anyone else. But this is also a truism, because
obviously they would prefer to be anywhere with their crush than with
someone else, especially if it's a dance or party. So what's the difference between prom night and other occasions? Prom night comes at
the end of the year, whether it's junior or senior year; and it is this
tie-in with endings that makes all the difference. If it's at the end of
junior year (more crushes hook up junior rather than senior year),
then you are returning to school in the fall with a bf or gf, and this is
a status thing, as if to say that you are capable, mature enough, eligible, and, clearly, desirable. The proof is that you are taken. If it's at
the end of senior year, then it's all of the above plus the knowledge
that this is your last opportunity to hook up with your crush while still
in high school. These are two very powerful forces driving teens and
they come together in prom. On the one hand they have to do with
coming of age—proving yourself through advertising your sexual
maturity by selecting a mate (however temporary that partner later
turns out to be). On the other, they have to do with endings—the end
of high school as a stage in life and the beginning of another stage.
Prom night crystallizes these two forces, thus spurring teens to action.

Spontaneous and Private

The next four chapters are about crushes asking each other to prom. In this first chapter, the asking characteristically takes place without an audience and without preparation, or with very, very minimal preparation. What makes these stories special is how spontaneous the moment of asking is. The person either blurts out their request with virtually no forethought, or circumstances work out in such a way that the asking "just happens." This spontaneity is most effective when the two people have secret, long-time crushes on each other but are afraid to make their feelings known. Asking the person to prom provides an excellent excuse for overcoming this fear. Although more than 70% of the people who get asked to prom wait until prom night to hook up into serious couples, more than 90% of those who ask spontaneously also start going out that day or very shortly thereafter. That's because for these kinds of askings, the moment of asking someone to prom and the moment of asking the person out, are one and the same.

Manet, Hoover High, Glendale CA

Well actually, I had this crush on him and didn't know what to do…so I just finally decided it didn't matter whether he liked me or not. If he didn't it wouldn't be a big deal cuz after high school I wouldn't even see him anymore. We were at snack and I said "r u gonna go to prom?!" and he said, "I don't know…no one's asked me and there's one girl I wanna go with but I'm afraid to ask cuz I don't know if she likes me!" So then I said, frowning, "Oh…Well I hope she says yes…If I were her I would, ur too cute for her not to!" I was about to walk away when he hugged me from behind and said, "Go to prom with me! Ur the one I wanted to ask!" And he turned me around and kissed my cheek! It was the cutest thing in the world!! Oh, and now we're "kinda goin out!" and I can't stop smiling every time I think about him!

Grace, Westerville North HS, Westerville OH

I had been in love with this guy for like two years, and finally I was getting the courage to ask him to my prom. I saw him when he was all by himself, so I went up to him, and started to ask him, but on my way, I tripped and spilled my chocolate milk all over myself! It was sooo embarrassing, but to make it worse, I have a retainer, and that flew out of my mouth. It hit his shoe. I wanted to die, but then he picked it up, and handed it to me. He had a retainer too! I knew right then that we were meant for each other. I didn't even have to ask him, he asked me! It was the greatest day of my life. We went to prom and had so much fun, and now we have been dating for two weeks!

Cassidy, RCHS, Clayton GA

Well, I was really crushing over this guy, but I knew that he wasn't good for me and that he would hurt me. One of my friends started fooling around with him knowing that I liked him. I started crying in class and there was this other guy that always asked me if I was ok, which was really sweet, but I didn't know his name (he was in my 5th period class). One day at lunch I was sitting at the table with my friends and the 5th period guy came over and sat with us, but he didn't really talk. All of us girls started talking about prom and I said, "I wish I could go to prom!" And then my friend looked over to the guy (I'll call him E) and back at me and said, "Why don't u go with E!" I was like, "No, he doesn't even know me!" But then E looked at me and got this little smile on his face and said, "That's a definite possibility!" That day in class, I started crying again because me and the guy that I liked had had a little argument. I went to the back of the room and sat down beside E. E leaned right over and whispered into my ear, "I'll treat you better than that other guy ever could. Will you go out with me?" I was totally in shock and I got a HUGE smile on my face, thought for a second, and said yes!!! We've been together for just about 8 months now and I couldn't be happier. I really think I've found the greatest of men and he's all mine! And he kept his promise and has NEVER hurt me and there is no doubt in my mind that he ever will!!! Plus we are going to prom. :P

Desiree, Jackson High, Jackson MI

I started chilling with this guy a couple of weeks before prom. Every day, as it got closer to prom, he would get more nervous around me, like he didn't know what to say. I wanted to ask him what was wrong, but one of my girlfriends said it's a guy thing. So I tried to ignore it. It just didn't work. I went up to him a week before prom and asked him why he was acting so different. We were standing in front of McDonald's at the time, and he said, "I want to ask you something." I was kind of worried, but didn't think anything of it. Then he said, "I know we only started hanging out a few weeks ago, but I was wondering...." He was building up too much suspense and I was really getting worried now. We both had feelings for each other, and we both knew it—we wrote love poems to each other every day in school. Then finally, he said, "Will you go to the prom with me?" I cried a little, and said, "I would be honored." He gave me our first kiss and right then we knew we were going out.

Jennifer, REVHS, Redlands CA

I was talking to my friend on the Internet late one night and I asked him if he could call me because I needed his advice on something. He called me and I told him there was this guy that I wanted to go to prom with because I thought we would have so much fun since we get along really well, and that I thought I liked him but I wasn't sure because I wasn't sure if the feeling was returned. He asked me if he was the guy and I said yes. So he told me he liked me too. He said, "Do you...have any...uh...questions you want to ask?" I said, "Yeah. Are you going to prom with anyone?" He said, "No, not yet." I said, "Do you want to go with me?" I've liked him for almost two years...my heart was pounding so loud I'm surprised he couldn't hear it through the phone. To my surprise he said, "Yes." We've been hanging out a lot and talking a lot more now, and it looks like we're going to go out. But it was great. I went to bed very happy that night and now I can't wait 'til prom.

Amanda, Claymont, Uhrichsville OH

One night, a few friends showed up where I work, and one of the guys wanted to ask me to prom but he was kinda shy. So I went on my break and went and sat down and started talking to my friends. Everyone was hinting at the fact this guy wanted to ask me. So we were talking about the cute key chain my friend had and "the guy" picks it up to read it. He reads the first half then looks at me and says, "Amanda, will you go to prom with me?" And then he looks away and finishes reading the key chain! It was so cute!

Melissa, Youngstown OH

I was in English class when the guy I really dig came up and sat beside me. I was looking through his agenda (a school must) and I noticed he had "Prom Committee" written next to one of the days. So on the top of the day that had that writing, I wrote... "Ask Melissa to..." Then I scratched out "committee." The next week, on the date I had marked, he asked me to prom. I really didn't think he would, but he did!

Bek Song-Hwa, Lone Peak High, American Fork UT

I'm on the school's color guard and I was practicing. I was having a particularly bad day so I was venting by throwing some parallels (that's when the flag rotates above your head parallel to the ground). My guy friend was watching me. I had been really mean to him early that day— I hadn't talked to him and I blew him off when he asked what was wrong. Anyway, I threw a parallel and it hit me right in the eye. I was in such shock that I didn't start crying for about a minute, and when I touched my eye, it was smarting like crazy. I didn't know it at the time, but I had the ugliest black eye. My friend took me out into the hall and tried to calm me down. I did, after a little bit. While he was hold-ing me, he whispered in my ear, "Will you go to prom with me?" So I got asked while I had a black eye, mascara running down my face from crying, and was in the arms of the best person I know!

Kailua, Kalaheo HI

This guy that I kind of liked picked us up from school. I had gotten asked three times to prom already, but I didn't want to go with two of them, and the third guy was in boot camp. While we were in the car, my best friend said really loudly, "So, what are you doing for prom?" I smiled, and her sister yelled, "She's staying at home all alone because she doesn't have a date." I was so embarrassed. I told them that they both sucked, and began staring out the window. Then Mike, our ride, turned around and was like, "Why aren't you going to prom?" I looked at him and said, "Because you won't take me, Mike." He smiled and asked if I wanted him to take me, and I nodded. The conversation switched to what we should wear. I smiled the entire week...I'm still smiling.

Angel, Winston-Salem NC

My friends and I went to a restaurant one night. It was one of those places where you can write on the tablecloth because it was made of paper. We were having fun writing messages to each other and drawing little pictures, when I noticed that my "friend" (the guy I like) was kinda quiet. After a while he picked up a crayon and started to draw. He wrote lines and asked me to play hangman. I didn't really catch on to what he was doing until the last moment when I realized he had spelled out, "Will you go to prom with me?" It was one of the sweetest things anyone has ever done and I found myself totally speechless, but I put a huge smile on my face and nodded my head yes.

Annie, Green Hope High, Cary NC

I sit next to one of my guy friends in Spanish class, and we were learning how to invite people to do things. You can imagine how amazed I was when he said to me, "¿Quieres acompanarme al baile formal?" or "Will you go to the prom with me?" Of course I said "¡Si!"

Anonymous, NBHS, New Braunfels TX

Well, I've had this HUGE crush on this one guy for forever and when I say forever I mean since third grade. Everyone had always told us we should go out but he always had some girlfriend or wasn't ready to be in a relationship. So after two years of worshiping him in junior high and getting nowhere, by my sophomore year I was ready to give up all hope. But then one of my friends told me he had asked her for my phone number. I went home all excited hoping he would call me, but he didn't for like three weeks. Then finally he called and invited me to go see a movie. But he made sure to add, "Just as friends." So I met him there and we sat together, but he didn't lay one finger on me. After the movie I was pretty P.O.ed. We were waiting for our parents to come and get us so we sat down on a bench. Suddenly, out of nowhere, he started pouring his heart out to me. He started telling me about how much he liked me and how he was trying to make me jealous by going out with other girls. He was practically crying his eyes out, saying that the only reason he hadn't asked me out before was because too many people had gotten involved and he thought I would say no. Well, even though most of that didn't make much sense, I was glad he said it. Then on a quick note he added, "Do you wanna go to our prom with me?" Then sorta joking he goes, "Or should we just cut to the chase and get married?" Needless to say we went together and have been going out ever since!

Jessica, HVHS, VA

Well I had met this guy through my older sister and even though he is a lot older we got along REALLY well. He invited me to go up to the lake with him and a few friends and my sister. Well we went up there and had a great time. He and I jumped off the cliffs together, holding hands, and swam in the lake and stuff. When we were leaving, everyone else had gotten off the boat and he took both my hands and pulled my chin up and said, "Hey, what would you say to going to prom with me?" I looked up at him and said, "I think I would have to say yes." I was sooo excited about going with him I tripped while I was getting off the boat and almost fell in the lake. We have been together since that day, going on six months in 10 days!

Planned and Private

In the chapter you just read, asking for the most part bubbles out, without prior preparation—or the preparation is minimal. This next chapter contains more elaborate, less spontaneous ways in which people have asked their crush to prom. The askers all spend more time preparing, which not only makes the asking more involved, but also more formal.

I decided where to place each story by asking myself, how much time and money does the asker (75% of the time, a guy) spend on the asking, and do they do it privately or publicly? The askers in the Spontaneous and Private chapter, as well as in the stories you are about to read, all do it privately. But the expense in time and money is greater in this next set than in the former.

On a cautionary note, greater expense does not automatically equal a better way of asking. As always, how you ask depends on how well you know the person and how confident you are that they will say yes. Choosing an overly elaborate, expensive, involved way, for example, could scare the askee off and earn you a no, instead of the anticipated yes.

Devonny, San Diego CA

Well, I'm a sophomore, and I have never been kissed before (it's not cuz I'm totally ugly or anything, I just haven't...) and I have known this guy for my entire life. We have been best friends for years, and he didn't know, but I have liked him for a long time. The only problem is that he's a senior, so I never thought that he would like me more than as a best friend. He's totally cute and very popular, so that just added to my uncertainty about anything ever happening between us. Well one day me and one of my good friends were talking and I told her that for my first kiss, I wanted to be kissed in the rain, ya know, the whole stringy hair and rain dripping off your nose deal. A few weeks after that (about two months before the senior prom) my best friend (the senior) told me during passing period that he wanted to talk to me about something at lunch. I assumed he wanted advice on what color corsage to get his date or something like that. I said sure, but was really bummed because the lunch area at our school is outside and everything was wet from the pouring rain. All the students were huddled beneath the part of the cafeteria that was covered. Well, when he saw me, my best friend (the senior) ran over to me, grabbed me by the hand, and pulled me into the rain. He then pulled me close to him, and asked me if I would go to his prom with him. I was so happy I couldn't say anything and just hugged him. When I pulled away, he leaned in and kissed me, right there in the pouring rain, in front of everybody. Well I found out later that he had also liked me for a long time. So that day, I got my first kiss just the way I wanted it, plus I got asked to prom.

Angie, Los Angeles CA

Before my boyfriend and I had started dating, my boyfriend, (who is also my best friend in the entire world) did the cutest thing to ask me to prom. At about 10:30 at night he left a dozen long-stemmed roses on my doorstep and rang the doorbell. When I got there he was gone but the roses were there with a note that said, "Ang~ I hope you enjoy the roses, I tried to find some as beautiful as you are but this is the best I could do! Love, Andy. P.S. Look at your garage." On the front of my garage was this huge sign that said, "Will you go to prom with me?" The sign was sooo gorgeous, and when he drove back to my house five minutes later I ran over to him and gave him a big kiss. He said, "So I guess that's a yes?" That's also the night we started dating.

Tracy, SLO High, San Luis Obispo CA

I had been crushing on this guy since sophomore year, but had barely talked to him. At the beginning of the second semester, the only class I didn't have with him was the elective, when he was an office aid. Because we were now in classes together, we began to talk a lot and I mentioned to him my love of chocolate. Two months before the senior prom, I went to my locker to get a book out. When I opened my locker, hundreds of little Hershey's Kisses fell out and spilled onto the ground around my feet. Hanging from a hook was a little card that read, "If I could make your dreams come true, fulfill your every need,

I would give the world to you, if you'd go to prom with me. I love you, and I want to be with you. ~Keith." I turned around to see him standing there, leaning against a locker, a huge smile on his face. Of course I said yes, and we started dating that same day.

Samantha

I was too afraid to walk up to the guy I like and plain out ask him to the prom so instead I went to a computer and opened up different Word documents. On the first one I wrote, "Are you going to the prom?" On the second, I asked, "Do you wanna go with me?" On the third I put, "OK" and on the last I put, "Cool." Then I asked him to help me on my computer and he read the first message, "Are you going to the prom?" He said, "Maybe." I showed him the one that asked if he wanted to go with me. He said, "Sure." And then I showed him the last one, "Cool." We have been together since.

Angelica, RMC, London ON

I'd been so excited about prom since elementary school! I'd been trying to decide on my dream dress, so I bought some prom magazines for ideas. At last I found the perfect dress and showed my friend Mike. He somehow got a hold of the magazine and glued a picture of my face onto the girl wearing the dress and his face onto the tux model standing with her. Then he wrote in a speech bubble above his head, "Angelica, will you go to prom with me?" and then one above my head saying, "Oh Mike, I'd love to!" It sounds corny, but it was so sweet. Obviously I said yes!

Kate, Heritage High School, Littleton CO

I'm a freshman, and when I first got to high school this awesome senior asked me out. We ended up going out for three months, but then broke up two days before Valentine's Day. We stayed friends, but it wasn't the same. Then things started getting better. He started calling a lot more, we talked online all the time, and we hung out EVERY day after school. Then, one day he came over to my house. He hadn't been over in a while so it was cool. We ended up getting online, which was boring cuz it was what we always did. Then he was like, "Go get me a pop from downstairs." I thought it was annoying because he should get his own pop. But he gave me a puppy dog look so I gave in. When I came back he said, "Be right back, I have to go to the bathroom." I was about ready to say, "You have to leave," because things were getting boring. Except, when he was in the bathroom, the screensaver popped up, saying, "Will you go to prom with me?" It was adorable!!! I'm always on the computer and so is he, so it was a perfect way to ask. I'm really excited!!!

Ryan, Watertown WI

I have this really good friend and she was over at my house one night. All night I had been complaining how my stomach hurt, so naturally she was a little concerned. After several hours I was like, "Kim, I really need you to take a look at my stomach. I think something's wrong." She thought this was a little weird but she said ok and I lifted up my shirt and I had written on my stomach, "Kimberly, will you go to prom with me?" She almost had a heart attack laughing and kept saying, "Yes." It was a great time.

Ashley, Beaverton High, Portland OR

Well, I had this huge crush on this guy that I met through my cousin, and so one night I was up at my cousin's house, and Andy (the guy) was there too. He really really likes Mountain Dew, the pop, so I took little sheets of paper and a six pack of mountain dew and I decorated each can with a different word (will...you...go to...prom...with...me?) and put it in my cousin's fridge. Then, when we were sitting down to a movie, I asked him to go get me something to drink. So when he walked into the kitchen, he opened the fridge and saw the cans there, and I could hear him laugh, and he ran out and gave me a huge hug and said yes! It was the cutest thing ever!

Pam, Millburn HS, Springfield NJ

Well, I had been crushing on this guy for months. It was getting to be around the time where everyone was finding dates for the prom. What was I going to do? My crush was very popular at school, and I wasn't. I thought for sure he was going to ask Taylor, the most popular girl in the school. Anyways, me and my crush are in the same AP English class period three. One day our teacher assigned us a project to do in groups of two. I don't know why, but my crush asked me to be partners. I assumed it was because I am "the smartest in the class." He asked me for my student agenda to make a date that we would be working together. I thought nothing of it and put it away once he'd written in it. I was so excited that he wanted to work with me! That night when I was looking to see what my homework was, I saw it!! It was his handwriting!!! Asking me to THE PROM! Why me? I was sooo excited! So I called him. I asked if he could come over to do the project tonight, instead of next week. He said yes and drove right over. While we were on the phone, I pretended that I had not found the note. When he opened the door to my house I jumped into his arms and said, "YES, I would love to go to the prom with you!" That was the best day of my life!

Lynn, West Chicago High School, Carol Stream IL

I really liked this guy for a while, and we even got to go on a school trip together. Well, while were on this trip, we started hanging out a lot more. So when we got back, we exchanged numbers and got to know each other better. We are both in choir, and he is a really good singer. So one day he gets in front of the whole choir, and says, "As you all know, this weekend is Mother's Day, and my mom really wants me to sing her favorite song to her." So he starts singing, "You're just too good to be true, can't take my eyes off of you." He gets through the first 2 verses, and he starts making up his own words. As he's singing, he's getting closer to me. Still making up his own words, he sings, "If I take you by the hand, and hope you'll let me be your man, will you go to prom with me?" While he does that he's gone down on one knee, and is holding my hand. Everyone went crazy, and of course I said yes! It still brings a bright smile to my face.

Sarah, Stellarton High School, Stellarton NS

Well yesterday was my birthday and my crush came and picked me up from school, which was really sweet. Then he took me down to the beach and opened the doors for me and everything, being all gentlemanly and stuff, and I had to laugh. Then he went and got something out of his trunk and came over to me. He was all nervous and said really quietly, "Ya know, I'd really like it if you'd go to my prom with me." I was so shocked all I could do was say, "mmm hmm" and nod my head slightly. Then he handed me a teddy bear that he had his grandmother make for me, and a card that said, "Happy Birthday." And the best part was, when I opened the card, there was a message saying, "Will you go out with me?" He literally had to catch me b/c I fell, I was so surprised. He's the sweetest guy ever!!

Jenna, CHS, AZ

My theme for prom was "Chinese," so I asked a friend from another school by buying fortune cookies. With toothpicks I pulled the fortunes out and wrote new ones asking him to prom. Then I decorated a to-go box and put them in it. It was a smashing hit!!

Jessica, Los Angeles High School, Los Angeles CA

I had heard there was this one guy that wanted to ask me to the prom, but I didn't know him very well. He started coming to church with me, and we became friends during the winter months. At the beginning of March I heard he wanted to ask me soon, before anyone else beat him to it, but I didn't know when. I saw him at church on Wednesday night and when we said good-bye, he said, "Have a nice trip to school tomorrow." I didn't understand what that meant, but I said, "Okay." The next morning, my mom came into my room and was like, "Wake up, there is something on your car." I went out there, and sitting on the hood there was a bouquet of thirty-four sweetheart roses and a note. The note turned out to be a poem, and he asked me to prom in the poem. It was the sweetest way to be asked to prom! That day I didn't see him at school because he was on a field trip. So I sent him a carnation that had a note on it that said, "YES!" I heard that when he got it he had the biggest grin on his face!

Anonymous, Calgary AB

I live in Canada and it was blizzarding like crazy outside. I had just finished my ball practice and was ready to go home. My friends at practice told me that there was a star in my bag with a note on it. Well, this star was the first of about twenty stars in a treasure hunt I had to do outside in the snowstorm. Finally, I had gotten the last clue and it told me to go home. When I got there, my bedroom floor was covered in starburst with letters and numbers on them and I had to spell a paragraph. At the end of the paragraph it said, "Look when the stars shine brightest," and then as I turned my light off once I was ready for bed, his name was on the ceiling above my bed in glow-in-the-dark stars. It was pretty sweet, especially because we were together in like grade 7 and we had our first kiss together, but then when he went to high school we drifted apart...until now! I can't wait to go.

Chad, Riverside High, Greenville SC

This girl that works with two of my friends is so cute! I have always wanted to get to know her better, but I have been too scared to ask her for her number. We flirt back and forth, so one night I went by her workplace right after she got off, and we were playing around wrestling with each other, and I told her she hurt my back. Feeling bad that she hurt my back, she went to help me to my car (as I faked a limp). As soon as we got outside, she found a line of roses from the front door of her work to my car, and written on my windshield, "The only thing hurt would be my heart if you said no." It went perfectly, and we are now happily together.

Rachel, Chicago IL

I opened my locker and there were two photos taped together, of him in a tux (from a wedding he went to) and me in a dress (from when I was bridesmaid at my auntie's wedding). They were taped together as if we were holding hands. On the back of them he'd written, "Please make this dream of mine come true?" So I did!!

Courtney, Hoover High School, Birmingham AL

I had liked Bryan for a long while before he started tutoring me in chemistry and algebra two days a week after school. Every day, before we began tutoring, he gave me a little quiz to see where I stood on all the information we were covering. Well, one Thursday he handed me my quiz and told me to get started, but said he had to go talk to a teacher. I started the quiz and did numbers one and two ok. But number three said, "Will you go with me to prom?" I reread it like four times to make sure I wasn't going crazy. Then I wrote, "Yes" in the answer blank and asked him if it was the right answer. He was like, "Yeah, that was the answer I was hoping for."

Emily

I had just moved (my dad's been transferred for the 8th time) to a new school. I had just left behind a guy I really liked, and was having a really hard time dealing with the fact that he and my best girlfriend had gotten together.

So I came to my new school for the first day, completely terrified and still a bit depressed. In my Spanish class there's this really nice guy named Scott. He sat beside me that first day and something about the way he talked to me made me feel right at home. He was kinda goofy, but totally fun to be around. Also, he had sort of longish hair— except that I hated that.

So a few months pass, and Scott is my best friend here. We do stuff every weekend, but not like a date, and he tells me about his girl problems, etc.

Well, prom is rolling around, and I am sure I won't be asked, since the only guy that spends any time with me is Scott, and he's already told me his elaborate plot to ask this gorgeous popular girl that he's liked forever.

Well, he asks me to hang on Friday night, as usual. So he comes to pick me up, and his hair is cut! He looks phenomenal!! We watch a romantic movie, and he doesn't make a move, so I figure it's just coincidence.

After the movie, he looks over at me and says, "Em, I don't know how to tell you this but I've been falling in love with you for the past few months, and everything about you makes me want to be better. Could you please come to the prom with me?"

With that, he pulls out a handpicked beautiful pink rose, and then kisses me very gently and sweetly on the lips.

Prom was amazing (and the popular gorgeous girl didn't even get asked!). Scott's still my best friend but now also my boyfriend.

Matt's Girl

This is my senior year, and I really really wanted to go to prom. There's this guy Matt that I've had a crush on for a while now...and I see him every day. We always flirt and stuff, but both of us are just flirty people, so I never thought he liked me when he flirted with me. So, of course, I was hoping that he would ask me to prom. Well, it was five weeks to prom, and he and I both didn't have dates...then four weeks, and then almost three weeks to prom! My friends all wanted me to go in their group for prom, so they were trying to set me up with another guy, but I was holding out for Matt. Then in school on Friday, he told me to call him Saturday when I was free so we could hang out (yay!). So I did, and he came to my house and picked me up. Then we were going to see a movie, but it didn't start for another hour and a half, so he said we could go somewhere to "kill some time." When I asked where we were going, he wouldn't tell me; he'd just say, "It's a surprise." So...the thought entered my mind that he might be asking me to prom...and I got REALLY excited. Then he pulled into a parking lot; the beach parking lot! We both got out of the car, and were walking down the path to the beach, and he suddenly said, "Oh wait! I was going to ask you something...." I was thinking, "This is it! He's going to do it!" And then he said, "...But I forgot what it was...ah, the question just left me! Hold on, let me try and remember it...." So of course I was going crazy, but tried to act calm...and when we got down to the beach, he said, big grin on his face, "Oh yeah...now I remember," and he was looking at the sand, and in HUGE letters it said "PROM?" I was blown away! I said yes and we hugged, and I nearly cried. Then he said he was sorry he'd waited so long, but he just couldn't think of the perfect way to ask me...and he'd been planning it for weeks. The prom was AMAZING, and we've been dating ever since then.

Heidi, Milwaukee MI

Last year, I was a sophomore. I had study hall every day with some
people in my grade, as well as some juniors. There was this one particular junior who I had such a huge crush on! He, of course, would
sit in the corner with his girlfriend and make out. She was gorgeous,
with a perfect body and a fantastic face. I had pretty much accepted
that I was never going to go out with this guy, but still I was interested,
and made some efforts to find out more about him. I soon learned
that his name was Brian, and that he was seventeen. All of my friends,
who knew my feelings, were trying to convince me to talk to him. One
day, I was out in the hall, walking to the bathroom, and I saw him
coming toward me. I totally surprised myself and said, "Hi, Brian."
Then he totally shocked me by saying, "Hey, Heidi," right back. I
could not believe he knew my name! After that day I started to talk to
him more and more during study hall. During this time, he broke up
with his girlfriend for being too pushy (so he said). His prom night
was coming up but he'd never said a word about it. One night though,
when I got home after school, I found Brian sitting on my living
room couch. He had a rose in his hand, and he said to me, "Heidi, I
noticed you the first time we were in study hall together. I always
wanted to talk to you, because you seemed like such an amazing person. Problem was my girlfriend would get really pissed off. I realized
that if I couldn't talk to someone when I wanted to, that things were
definitely wrong. That is why I broke up with her. The greatest day of
my life was when I started to talk to you. I found my best friend that
day. And if you will let me, I would love to say that I found my girlfriend that day. Will you go to the prom with me?" I was so happy to
hear this beautiful speech that I ran up and kissed him! That was my
first kiss, and on prom night, I have to say we shared many, many
more :)!!!

Arylle, MSU Billings, Great Falls MT

I had had some really bad relationships over the last couple of months
with two guys that were on-and-off. Those guys and I used to be really
great friends and then got involved and everything got messed up.
Well...prom was coming up and I thought I would be the only girl
without a date because I didn't really have anyone I figured cared for

me enough to ask me to prom. I had bought my dress when I was going out with the second on-and-off guy, and I had everything I needed for prom, except a date. I sat at home one night finishing a project that would be due next Monday. I fell asleep halfway through the project and woke up to find my room totally decked out in beautiful crimson silk, candles, a dozen roses, and two prom tickets on my pillow. Near the prom tickets was a note that read, "I'm sorry this took so long, but I've never had the guts to come to this level with you. You are amazing and I can't get you out of my mind. Please come to prom with me Arylle. —Matthew." I got up out of my bed and walked into the living room to find my best friend, whom I had secretly had a crush on for about eight years, sitting on my couch talking to my mom and dad. When I walked out I didn't know what to do but run over to him, give him a kiss on the cheek, and hug him. It meant the world to me that he cared for me enough to tell me how he felt and then take me to prom. He's my best friend and it was the best prom of my life. We've been together since my junior year in high school and I am now a sophomore in college at MSU Billings.

Planned and Public

In the last two chapters, the asking took place privately, between asker and askee and with no audience. Now and then, askers are confident enough in themselves, and in the askee's response, that they don't mind asking in public. Most of the time, they ask with only a few people looking on, usually friends and such. In a few cases, however (as you will read in this chapter and the next), the asking can be alarmingly public and gutsy—going up on stage in front of the entire school to do it, for example, or enlisting the aid of teachers or administrative personnel.

Susie, Armstrong HS, Plymouth MN

Well the way my date asked me to prom was like this. He knew how much I liked Disney and that I especially loved Cinderella. My friends even used to call me Cinderella. Well it was during choir practice about two months before prom. We had about 100 people in my choir class. My date got one of my friends in on it and had her come in and borrow one of my shoes. She said she wanted to prove to another friend that we wore the same size. But she ran off with it! I started to chase after her, but my choir director shooed me back into the choir room and told me we were starting choir, with or without my shoe. A few minutes into choir, this kid dressed in like medieval clothes threw the doors open and two trumpet players came out playing a trumpet concerto my date had composed. Then the "doorman," the medieval dressed kid, said, "Announcing... PRINCE CHARMING!" and my date entered the practice hall dressed in Prince Charming's outfit from Cinderella. He had my shoe on a pillow and did the whole, "I'm looking for the lady who wears this shoe." And then he found me in the rows and put the shoe on my foot and the shoe had a note that said "prom?" It was so cute, everybody cheered. I said yes, of course, and we got it all on video!

Anonymous, Murrieta Valley High, Murrieta CA

My crush asked me to the prom on the day of my birthday. In my first period class there was a cupcake on my table. Second period, a single long-stemmed rose. Third period, there was a basket with Hershey's Kisses on the bottom and a dozen roses on the top. To its handle were tied three balloons and a note that said, "Happy birthday." Fourth period I got a teddy bear. It had a sign saying, "I have a question for you." Fifth period a note said, "Please say 'yes.'" Sixth period another note, which said, "I can't wait to see you." Then finally in seventh period he was there, my crush, in my class, sitting in my chair. I walked to my seat and he got up. I was still standing, and he got on his knees in front of the class and the teacher and said, "I'd be delighted if you would do me the honor of going to prom with me." My best friend handed my crush a long-stemmed rose which he then gave to me.

Karen, TX

At our school, our morning announcements are done through the television, and students in the media class read the news. So one of my best friends was reading the announcements one morning and at the end, he said, "One more thing before we sign off," and he held up a posterboard that said, "Karen, you're my princess. Will you go to prom with me?" I saw him after that class, and of course I said yes.

Rachel, Denver CO

I have been good friends with Kyle all thru high school. Our freshman year we went to our homecoming dance together. He promised me that night that he would take me to prom when we were seniors. Anyway...Kyle and I went on a ski trip three weeks before prom. He said he would ski every trail with me, but he skipped out on one of them. I found him later at the chair lift. We rode up the mountain together, and in the snow on the hillside, in huge letters, he'd written, "Rachel, I never break a promise. PROM? LOVE, Kyle." He had drawn a heart next to the writing. I turned to him with tears in my eyes. He had a promise ring in his hand and asked to be with me. I said yes and we've been together for eight months. Promises kept are the best!

Melissa, St. John Edwards High, Minnetonka AK

I was really hoping that this one boy would ask me to prom. He was charming. I am the vaptain of the swim team and every day my team practices after school. Robert (the boy) decided to go to the swimming pool and fill the pool with rubber duckies. There were at least 500. On some of them there were letters, and I had to put them together in a puzzle that said, "Melissa, will you go to prom with me please? It would make me very happy." It took the entire swim team about two hours to put the ducky puzzle together. And when we did, I was so happy! So was the team, because we didn't have practice that day since it took so long to put the ducky puzzle together. YAY!

Laura, Clear Lake HS, Houston TX

This happened to one of my friends. We play varsity soccer, and we were playing our big rival, Brook. After the game (we all knew this was going to happen, but Christi, my friend, didn't) as we were walking off the field, seven guys ran out onto the field without their shirts on. They each had one letter of her name on their chest. They arranged themselves to make it spell Christi. Then they yelled, "Christi!" And each one jumped around one at time, and they had, "Will you go to prom with me?" written on their backs. Then they all ran over to the guy who was asking and started jumping around him. When they moved away, he was standing there all in black with a rose in his teeth. So she ran over, he gave her the rose and kissed her cheek, and of course she said yes!

Kelsey, RHS, CA

I was in guitar lab with this guy that I really liked. We're pretty good friends and I really wanted him to ask me to junior prom. One day, the teacher called on him to do his test, which was playing what he'd practiced on the guitar. He started out just strummin' the familiar song that we'd heard him practice over and over. When he was done, he surprised everyone by playing a second song and singing with it. He had written it especially for me, and in it he asked me to prom! It was so sweet because everyone had gathered around him and we were just like "awwww!"

Julia, FBA, Dallas TX

My study hall teacher wouldn't let anyone into the room so we all had to stand around in the hall. Well I went and asked him if I could go get a drink of water and he said, "Ya, but I want you to come in here first." So I started to walk off and he said, "No, I mean come into the room now." So I walked into the room and there were white balloons all over the floor, up to my knees! And on a table there was one red balloon shaped like a heart that said, "Pop Me!" So I popped it and there was a note inside that said, "Julia, will you go to Junior-Senior with me? Love, Matt." Plus there were roses next to the balloon! It was very much of a shock since me and this guy had only talked on the Internet and I was a freshman.

Judy, GA

I have a way good friend, Josh. He is just like my brother. I hadn't been asked to prom yet and we were talking one night on the phone and he told me he wasn't going to prom. Since I was our school's Prom Coordinator, I told him he had to go—that I had just made it a rule. At 2am that night an alarm started to go off in my room, and it wasn't my alarm clock. I found it after a few moments, and on the top of it was the letter "J." It turns out he had put 11 alarm clocks in my room, and they all went off between 2 and 3am, and each had different letters on each one. The last alarm clock said, "I hope it's not too late to ask: will you go to prom with me?" So I had to unscramble the 11 letters to figure out his name. Of course I said yes, and now we are together. He told me prom night that he had liked me for a long time, and I told him I had liked him. We've been going out since prom night!

Jazzy

It was two weeks before prom. He was your average perfect guy. The most popular guy in the school, who is one of those precious few that isn't totally full of himself. Totally cute, and kind of a jock. Our school's cafeteria has a huge stage on the far side of it. One day during the busiest lunch hour I was sitting at a table with a couple of my guy pals, when Mr. PerfectCuteJock got up on the stage. And of course, everyone shut up to see what he had to say. He said, "I know I'm late. To make up for it, I'm up here confessing that it took me this long to build up my courage. I figure that if I'm up here asking and making an ass of myself in front of all these people, it'll better my chances and make up for lost time." He looked straight at me, got down on one knee (the entire lunch room giggled), and said, "Will you go to prom with me?" I almost passed out.

Spectacular Asking

Ok, you'd better hang on to your seats. This is spectacular public asking. Guaranteed, most of us wouldn't dare.

Jenna, PHS, San Diego CA

I was asked to prom by my ex-boyfriend. One night my friends and I went to a football game. But right before half time started, all of the cheerleaders did a special cheer. They made five pyramids and each girl on top was holding a sign. Then they all held up their signs, which spelled out, "Will you go to prom with me Jenna?" Then everyone's eyes were directed toward the middle of the football field where my ex was holding two-dozen roses and a microphone. I made my way toward him and took the microphone in my hand and said yes. The entire crowd cheered.

Katie, IL

I went to a school play with the guy I liked, and as the cast came out to take their bows, he left, saying he had to go to the bathroom. I thought it was a little odd since the show would last for all of 30 seconds longer, but whatever. So after the cast left, the student director and student producer came out and said, "Wait, everyone, before you all leave, we have one more thing to say. The spring play means that it's springtime, and love is in the air...and it's also PROM SEASON." Then they started calling my name, and I went up on stage, and I was really nervous but excited. And a lot of my close friends were sitting in the front row, and I could see their faces. And the guy I liked came out from backstage with a single red rose in his hand and said, "Katie, will you go to prom with me?" and I said, "Of course," and gave him a huge hug. We walked off the stage and all our friends scrambled to come backstage and congratulate us while everyone else clapped like crazy. It was the most amazing night of my life.

Ginger, West Springfield High School, Springfield VA

We were going to see Michael's little sister's play at the middle school at 7pm. I had just gotten a new car so Michael said he really wanted to drive. I agreed, and when we arrived he parked in front of the school (which was a fire hazard), and he said he just wanted to stay here a minute and tell me some things he had on his mind. He explained how a friend of his was doing drugs and that he wanted to help him but didn't know what to do. Well, we had this "deep conversation" about that "friend" for about 15 minutes. Next thing I know there is a cop behind us with his lights on. Just recently Michael's license was suspended for a speeding ticket (or so he told me), so I got incredibly nervous. The cop was a real jerk. He took both our licenses and when he came back from his car he asked Michael to "step out of the vehicle." So he did, and he spread him as I watched from the passenger seat. A bag of "weed" was thrown on the car from Michael's pocket. My mouth dropped. Michael is NOT one to do something like this at all—although I suddenly understood about his "friend." I was then asked to step out of the car. The cop escorted me to his car. By this time there was a crowd gathering around us. Michael had already been handcuffed and was sitting on the side of the curb. The cop told me to get in the back of the car and so I did. I'm crying by this point and I look over to see a HUGE sign on the seat: "GINGER, PROM?" I SCREAMED! I ran out and pushed Michael while the cop says to me, holding the bag of "weed," "Would you like some oregano?" I couldn't believe it. After getting out of my shock stage, I said yes, I would go with him. Later, Michael took me to his house, where flowers and sparkling cider were waiting for me. What a night!

Kate, Chicago IL

We have this huge club where anywhere from thirty to over a hundred people show up on Wednesday nights to hang out at our school. I desperately wanted this senior guy who I liked but never thought I had a chance with to ask me to prom. Though I got to know him really well, we hadn't talked much for a while. Anyway, he got all the people who were at the club that night in on this, and made sure I was going. He filled the room with candles (I'm obsessed with scented candles) and spelled out "Prom?" in candles on the floor. I walked in and didn't realize what was going on at first, but then said, yes, of course! and I kissed him for the first time—in front of everybody!

Angel, Devon AB

It was the day of the Christmas parade and classes were cancelled in the morning because of the school's participation in the parade. I hadn't been asked to the prom yet, but I had been talking to this SUPER HOTT guy and I really wanted to go with him. He called me up the day of the parade and asked me to go watch it with him. As we were watching, the float made by the grocery store which he worked at came by. He pointed it out and I looked. On top of the float there was this huge heart-shaped sign that said, "Angel, will you go to the prom with me?" Needless to say we went to the prom and have been going out ever since.

Haley, NV

Well, it was a pep assembly and the entire school was there, and I got asked to go down to the gym floor. As I'm walking down, the four captains of the football team are bringing out a baby pool filled with Jello and tiny little hollow balls. "Now, you're being asked to prom Haley, and the name of the boy who is asking you is in one of those balls...so I'd get looking!!!" says Adam, the student body president. The whole time I'm looking, the pep-assembly is still going on around me. So it's the end of the assembly and I still haven't found the right ball. "Sorry, Haley, I guess you can't find a date!!" says Adam. "Well," he adds, "I guess you'll just have to go with me!!" Yes it was him the whole time! He then had his friend come out with a dozen roses and a balloon...yeah he was pretty tricky, but you should hear how I answered him!! :-)

Boyfriends and Girlfriends

(Bfs-Gfs)

The next two chapters are all about boyfriends-girlfriends (bfs-gfs) asking each other. You'll notice as you read that the ways in which bfs-gfs ask is at least as romantic as crushes. It is also as outrageous and involved, if not more. This tells us that the process of asking is an integral part of prom, and that you can't really think of prom without including this process (and all the preparation and excitement that goes with it). Consider this story, for example:

> My boyfriend had automatically assumed that we were going to prom together-which we were—but I had secretly hoped he'd ask me anyway. We were trying to figure everything out...limo ride, motel room, my dress, his tux, tickets...and he completely forgot to ask me. I wasn't going to make a big deal over it, though. But my friend told him one day that he had one prob-lem about prom—he didn't have a date. He was confused, and she told him that he had never asked me, so he didn't have a date. He was so embarrassed and apologetic and he asked me to go with him right then and there. He was all stumbling over his words because he felt badly and suddenly got very shy, but of course I said yes! :-)
> **(Katie, Braintree MA)**

This story sums up the need to be officially asked to prom, which means that asking is not an option, but a necessity, and therefore a fundamental part of the overall prom experience.

On the next pages, we have boyfriends and girlfriends formally asking each other to prom. I have broken the stories down into two chapters: Bfs-Gfs Asking in Private and Bfs-Gfs Asking in Public.

B∫s-G∫s Asking in Private

Perhaps the most romantic ways of asking are typically done in private. It isn't the fear of rejection or that everyone will know or laugh that makes someone ask privately. It is the need for candles and music and special, highly personal stagings. And this can only take place more privately—like all deep romance. In the stories below, it is boyfriends and girlfriends asking each other to prom. Because they are already hooked up, they can afford to be deeply romantic in the ways that they ask each other—and some of them certainly take advantage of this romantic possibility.

Nell, Los Angeles CA

My boyfriend and I have been together for a very long time. I love him very much, and next year we are getting married :-). When I was a freshman in high school, we were dreaming about prom together, lol—we are the romantic type, and some friends say we might just be the corniest romantics around. He always had wanted to go to prom with me, and I with him. Two weeks before prom, I found a note on my bedroom window. It said, "Follow the music." At first I was a little puzzled because I didn't hear any music, so I opened my window, and I heard this beautiful music, coming from the beach. I went downstairs, and out my front door, and after ten feet or so, I realized I was stepping on rose petals, a long path of them down to the beach, and so I got very excited, with the biggest smile. As I reached the end of the path of petals, the words of the song got clearer:

> Whoa! My love, my darling, I hunger for your touch.
> Alone. Lonely time. And time goes by, so slowly,
> And time can do so much. Are you still mine?
> I need your love.

I almost cried, it was so romantic—"Unchained Melody" is one of our favorite songs. I reached the beach and he was standing there, in the headlights of his car, and I ran to him, and threw my arms around him, and asked him what it was all about. He replied, "Go to prom with me?" And I said, "Yes! Yes of course!" And we waltzed around on the beach, and we had fun just laughing, and shedding a few tears enjoying the moment. :-)

Chelsea

While me and my boyfriend were snowboarding at a local ski moun-tain, he told me to go off the course and follow him up this one path that he had made. I followed the path through these big pines (might I add we were in the middle of nowhere). We came to a stop, and in a clearing between the pines a blanket lay on the snow. On it, hot cocoa in a thermos and two-dozen red roses were waiting for me. One of the roses was yellow. While I was standing there looking, amazed, he turned his head to look in the snow and my eyes followed his. Written in the snow was, "I love you with all of my heart, will you go to prom with me?" With tears in my eyes I hugged him. He took my face in his hands and kissed me on the forehead. He is my fairytale come true!!!!!!

Michelle, Clear Lake High School, Houston TX

He wasn't asking me but my best friend, and I was helping him out. He started out by taking her to a romantic dinner theater, just for a date. But on their way home he called me and my friends and gave us the code word to go and set up for his asking her to prom. So we went to their "spot" at a park bench next to a local pond. The night before, her boyfriend had brought me all the necessary materials. When we got there, we laid a white sheet over the bench, and set a CD player under it playing her favorite love songs. Then we spread three Kroger bags full of rose petals all over the ground and bench, along with a dozen daisies (her favorite flowers). Then we put forty candles around the bench, in the cupholder, and along the top of the bench. Then we placed the formal poem he had written her on the bench. At last, we ran away when they drove up. It was so beautiful and romantic! She said yes, then he asked her to dance right there, and they danced under the moonlight =) It was so sweet!!!!!

Ben's Extremely Lucky Girl, Antigo High School, Antigo WI

One night I went over to his house and he asked me to come into his room, and on his bed was a pile of teddy bears that aren't usually there. As I sat down, I saw that one of them had a certificate that said its name was Ben, and that he belonged to me. He then handed me this adorable white bear with a red bow, and when I grabbed it by the paw, it said, "Ann Marie, will you go to prom with me?" Of course I said yes! He had ordered a bear that had his voice recorded in it, and now, whenever I'm having a bad day, I get re-asked to my junior prom.

Rachel, Acalanes, Lafayette CA

My boyfriend of three months left a trail of Reese's peanut butter cups in my hallway that spelled out, "WILL YOU…" that led to my bed and up to the gorilla stuffed animal that he gave me for my birthday. The stuffed gorilla was sitting there holding a framed sign that said, "Go to prom with me?" It was so sweet!!!

Lauren, Fairfield High, Cincinnati OH

My boyfriend made a calendar with all our pictures and movie ticket stubs and other memorabilia, and in the month of March it said, "Prom?" in big, fancy writing.

Dana, Kennedy High School, Denver CO

The prom was coming up and I knew my boyfriend was gonna ask me but I just didn't know when. I'm in band, and one day it was a block band, which I hate with a passion and he knows it. I open my case and at first glance I am like, "Who put this trash in my case?" And then I recognize his handwriting. So there's a ton of Post-it notes on either side of this folded white paper. Each Post-it note had written on it something that he loved/liked about me, or just something nice in general. I dug through these, reading (and smiling) as I went, and finally got down to a large white piece of paper at the bottom of the case. I was expecting to be asked when I opened it…but it was blank. It just said, "If this burns, tell me…" (?!?!) And there was an arrow saying, "Start here." I was totally confused, but later found out he had written the msg in lemon juice and I had to hold it over a flame for a little bit so that the letters would come out. Sweet, huh?

Courtney, Rosary High School, Placentia CA
Ok, so I was seeing this guy and I really wanted him to ask me to prom, but he was taking FOREVER!!! So one night when I was grounded, his best friend called me and asked me if I would be home that night. Since I was grounded, I said yes and asked him why. He said he wanted to come over and play Nintendo. I thought it was kinda weird, but whatever. So I said "Sure, come over around 7pm." So around 7pm, there was a knock at the door. I went downstairs in my pajamas and there was no one at the door. I looked down and there was a rose on my porch. I walked outside, and on each step, there was another rose. There were 11 roses leading down the steps and down the walk, and the twelfth rose was being held by my boy, who was sitting on his car. I walked over to him and he's like, "Will you go to prom with me?" I wanted to cry, I was so happy.

Lexy, St. Lloyd's, San Francisco CA
First he asked me out to the movies. I accepted, and on the night of the "movie date" he picked me up in—get this—a horse and buggy! We drove—er—rode right past the movie theatre! I asked where he was taking me and all he said was, "You'll see." Then I asked why he had brought his boombox, and he said nothing. Finally we got there. "There" was on a highway beside a forest! I asked, "Is this some sort of joke?" He laughed and said, "Follow me." We walked for about ten minutes and there before me was the most beautiful waterfall I had ever seen! He got out a rose and placed it in my hair. He asked me then. He said, "Lexy, would you do me the honor of escorting me to the junior prom?" Stunned, I paused for a few beats before answering, "Of course!" And he kissed me on the lips for a long time. "But why did you bring your boombox?" I asked. He set it on a rock and pressed play. We danced for hours! It was the most romantic night of my life...so far!

Bʄs-Gʄs Asking in Public

In these stories, the romance is still there as boyfriends and girl-friends ask each other to prom, but the person asking decides to make a big deal of it. A moonlit evening with candles or a beach at sunset is not enough; and so he or she asks in front of friends, or in front of the whole school. Not that any other way of asking isn't also a big deal. It's just that some people need an audience.

Britney, Keller High School, Keller TX

Well, this is how I got asked to prom. I went to Six Flags two weeks before prom. I really like those planes that fly by with announcements and stuff like that on them. Well when I went to Six Flags, I heard one and I looked up and there was my name! The flag had a big, "Will you go to prom with me, Britney? Brandon E." Then I looked down and there was Brandon! It was sooo cute! Of course I said yes! Then when I went to prom we were dancing and he took me off to the side and gave me a rose! Then he told me to play "he loves me he loves me not," and when I did there was a silver ring and a diamond in the middle of the rose! Then he got on his knee and proposed to me! We've been married for 3 years now and I will always remember that day!

Meagan, Moapa Valley High, Overton NV

My boyfriend asked me to prom while I was on a bus on my way to Reno for state basketball. I was on the bus with about fifty other people—I'm on the dance team so we sat up front and the basketball team sat towards the back. Anyway, our coach started handing out candy bars that said, "Here she is, Meagan Brammer," on the front of the bar, but done so that it looked like "Hershey's." I got mine first and I said, "Hey, it has my name on it!!" I thought that everyone was getting candy bars with their names on it, but then I heard a big "Aaaaaawwwwwwwwwww" from the team behind me. It hit me—the candy bar wasn't from our coach, and I looked over at one of my teammate's candy bar and it too had my name on it!! Another girl told me to look at the back, and it said, "VITAL STATISTICS: MY DEAR SWEET—WOULD YOU PLEASE GO TO PROM WITH ME?" Then it had the candy barcode, and below that it said, "INGREDIENTS: "SUGAR AND SPICE AND EVERYTHING NICE." Then below that, it said, "MFD. BY JONATHAN." It was sooooooooo cute!! I was very excited. My face turned bright red and everyone took pictures!! Then about five minutes after that, my coach came back with a teddy bear that said, "I THINK YOU ARE 'BEARY' SWEET!! HAVE FUN UP AT STATE!!—JON" It was very cute!! I loved it to death!! He's the best ever!!!

Anonymous, Rolling Meadows HS, Arlington Heights IL

Well I asked my girlfriend to prom on May 1st, last school year. What I did was...I had a 12 ft x 5 ft banner and I wrote her name on it very huge with two arrows underneath it pointing down. I called my friends, her friends, acquaintances, etc., and was able to gather about 45 people at the front of our school at 6:45 a.m. one morning (school starts at 7:25). Well we went to the edge of the road in front of school and everyone gathered around the sign in a half circle, with a few people holding the sign. The two arrows pointed down to a box that had once held a sink. I had spray-painted the word 'BABY' all over the box and taped a folded posterboard on top. I arranged for her mother to let her out at the front of the school that morning, instead of into the yard on the side as usual. She was very confused and looked all over for me. She opened the posterboard and it had a Dr. Seuss-like poem that I had written for her and a picture of us making a goofy face. Then she opened the box and I came out holding a Build-A-Bear. I pressed a button on the bear and it said, "So what'll it be, baby...will you go to prom with me?" It was fantastic...and it made the yearbook!

Angel, AHS, Anadarko OK

My best friend and I started dating like two months before prom. We were eating dinner one night and he leaned over and said something to his best friend, who then leaned over to my best friend and said something to her. They both then left the room, saying they were going to get everyone something to drink. They came back and handed everyone a glass. Mine had a note on it. I opened it and it said, "You have been my best friend for three years, and now you're the love of my life, will you please go to prom with me?" It was signed, "Your true love, J.M.G." I was so shocked!! I started crying and said yes!!!!!!!

Andrea, Blackfoot High School, Blackfoot ID

I have been dating this guy for about four months, and I really liked him and we have a lot of fun together. We go to different schools, and what makes it even better is that both schools are rivals. So, everywhere we go we get harassed for being with each other because of the different school thing. Well, I was at my boyfriend's homecoming football game and I couldn't find him anywhere on the field. Normally, he starts, being a defensive line backer, so I was starting to get worried. All of a sudden I hear, "Can I have your attention please?" I turn around and listen. Then I see this big burly football player (my bf!) running up towards the stands with a dozen roses—in front of his entire school! Up on the billboard I see written, "Andrea, will you go to prom with me?" I was so embarrassed! But us being from different schools, it was the most wonderful thing he could've done. How could I resist?!!

Kristin, Central High, Canada

I recently started dating this guy in grade 12. Seeing as how I'm in grade 11, I was kinda nervous because grad (or prom for Americans) was coming up soon. We had been together for about two months, and just last Monday I got a wonderful surprise. I went to my first class of the day and sure enough, sitting on my desk was a rose. But here's the deal...there was nothing else. Not a note, not anything. I asked my teacher about it and she claimed to know nothing at all. When she started teaching the lesson, she wrote something on the board. I wasn't really paying attention, but then again who does in math? The girls in my class started giggling and saying, "awww, too cute" stuff. I looked up, and my teacher had written, "Kristin, the first time my eyes met yours I knew you needed to be my girl. From…??" I was kinda confused, cuz I figured if it were from my boyfriend he would have just put his name. I made my way to my second class of the day and sure enough, another rose lay on my desk. Once again the teacher wrote another note on the board. Once again it said, "From…??" This continued until lunch when I went to where I normally hang out. There, dressed in a suit and tie was my boyfriend, waiting on bended knee, with the rest of a dozen roses and a HUGE sign behind him that said, "You're my girl at last, but will you be my girl for grad?" He also had a CD player playing our song in the background. I was SOOOOOOO embarrassed because there are three thousand people at my high school and it seriously felt like everyone was watching….Well, to finish my story, I'm a little crybaby. My heart totally melted and I ran up and gave him a big kiss!! Sweetest guy ever!!

Katie, Carlsbad High School, Oceanside CA

I went out to my car one morning before school. I found twenty or so bananas just chillin' in there. No note, no anything. Confused, I went to school thinking that my boyfriend had a part in it. I called him at break and asked him. He said, "No," and sounding bummed, he said he wanted to surprise me later, but that it probably wouldn't work out. Well it worked, because after lunch I went to my car and there was my guy, dressed in a gorilla costume holding a sign that said, "I'd go bananas if you went to prom with me." It was hilarious and I can't wait to ask him to mine!

Sandy, Dallas TX

I came back from lunch with all of my friends like I do every day, and walked to where everyone hangs out. My friends and I were standing by a wall, and my back was to it. All of a sudden everyone was looking up and then a ton of red rose petals sprinkled down on me. I turned around and looked up and my boyfriend was on the roof of the building. He was holding a sign that said, "Sandy, will you go to prom with me?"

Ann Marie, ThunderRidge, Littleton CO

I've been a lifeguard for the past three years so when my boyfriend wanted to come swim one night that I was working I didn't think anything of it. As I was up on the stand I saw him take his shirt off, and written on his chest was, "Will you go to prom with me?" He went tanning earlier that day for 40 minutes and used sticky letters to write it on his chest! Now, three months later, you can still read it, haha :-D

Jean, Rosemount High School, Rosemount MN

At Rosemount, prom is usually just for juniors and seniors unless they ask you...and I had been seeing this senior, Joe, for about 4 months. My two best friends were dating two of his good friends, and one day after school, we were all talking about going to prom. All the guys except Joe were talking about it and it made me think that he didn't want to go. The next day at school, I walked into my first hour class and there were Hershey's Kisses going from the door to my desk, and Kisses all over my desk and all round the floor. On my desk were a dozen roses and a sign that said...I'll kiss the ground you walk on if you'll go to prom with me...love, Joe. It was sooo sweet!!!

Truly Beautiful Moments

Sometimes, simply asking someone to prom is not enough. The process of asking becomes so charged with beauty that (as far as I am concerned) it qualifies for a category of its own. And so this chapter contains what I call "truly beautiful moments." They all have in common that a girl's dream is saved from descent into nightmare; that she's rescued from the brink of destruction, as it were. But isn't that what the best fairy tales are all about? Cinderella is saved from a horrible life. Snow White is saved from a wicked stepmother. Sleeping Beauty is saved from an eternal sleep. Their saviors are all eleventh hour prince charmings—and there's something about these eleventh hour rescues that sticks in our minds and hearts as somehow more beautiful than all of the rest.

Kelia, St. Lawrence High, Hemlock NY

It was two weeks before the prom when I finally admitted to my friends that I was still dateless. Everyone was shocked. I was the one in our group who had their dress picked out since freshman year and who had always made the biggest deal out of prom. Of course they all made fun of me. The only one who said nothing was my one friend Andrew. He told me that I shouldn't feel bad because I was a great person and that someone would eventually ask me, but that they were probably too shy or they would have asked already. For the next week still no one asked me. My friends began to quiet down and started pitying me. But Andrew still would tell me every day that I would probably get asked, that the person was just too shy. Finally, four days before the prom, I was crying in my room when my mom called for me to come downstairs. Hesitantly, I went down, my eyes still stained with tears. My mom smiled at me and told me to go into the living room, that someone was there to see me. I walked in and to my surprise Andrew was sitting there. I tried to smile but was just too sad. He didn't say anything, just stood up, and handed me a gift. Then he left. When I opened it, I started crying again, but for a different reason. Inside was a book with a picture of me on it. I looked through it, and there were pages covered with handwritten poems, with pictures of me and him with our other friends, and reasons for why I was special. On the very last page was a necklace with a note saying, "I'm sorry it took so long, but no matter how hard I looked I couldn't find a word to describe you. And then it came to me." On the back of the book was a name. "My Helen of Troy." We went to the prom and have been dating since.

Alexa, New York, NY

It was two weeks before prom and I was getting depressed. All my friends had dates, except me. I had a huge crush on this guy Josh. He was the popular type; he knew everyone and was sure to go to the prom with some hot blonde. Josh and I always got along well, and in our last year of high school we became really good friends, but more like I was his little sister type of deal—he always called me that, because we were such good friends. Anyways, I really wanted to ask him, but I heard that he had already found a date. I was so upset! I cried in my room on the last week before prom. On prom night, I went with my friends and their dates. Alone, I felt like a loser. I remember all my friends getting helped out of the limo by their dates. I had gotten out first, without being helped, and then I waited. One of my friends said, "Go in, we'll catch up." I shook my head no—I felt stupid going in by myself. I also didn't want to go in just yet because we were a little early. But my friend urged me to go. So I walked into the lobby of the hotel where our prom was being held. There, I stopped just inside the door, because, "Alexa, would you be my prom date?" is what I heard. It was Josh. He had planned this from day one, to surprise me and trick me into thinking he had a date. Of course I said yes, and I couldn't help it, I cried. He kissed my head and took my hand. I thought I was dreaming! That night, Josh asked me out. And ever since, we have been dating...four years now.

Kristin, State College High School, State College PA

Last year, I was so excited about my upcoming prom! All my friends had gone the year before and I'd heard all their stories, so this year I was finally going to have my own stories. But prom got closer and closer and I still had no date. I vented to my best friend Nathan every day. I thought there was maybe something wrong with me. He just kept smiling and telling me, "Good things come to those who wait." I honestly got kind of mad at him because he was being so optimistic, if not actually laughing at my distress. The night before the prom, my mom and I were talking about what I should do with a dress—I had already bought it—and no prom date, when she smiled and said, "Hey, when I came home from work today, this was on the porch." She handed me a teddy bear with a beautiful necklace around its neck, and it was holding a rose and an envelope. When I opened the letter, it said, "Don't worry, you're going to the prom. Be ready for me at 5 o'clock in full prom attire." My mom had no idea who it was from but still suggested I follow the instructions and see what happened. So the next day I got completely ready for the prom and waited. At exactly 5 o'clock, our doorbell rang. I closed my eyes, took a deep breath and walked down the steps. And at the bottom of my steps was Nathan standing in a tux holding a matching bracelet to the necklace I had gotten the night before. Naturally, I started crying and gave him a huge hug. As we were hugging, he whispered in my ear, "I told you good things come to those who wait," and kissed me on the cheek. It was just like a movie and I know I'll never be able to repay him for that night.

Colleen

From the first time I met Tom there was something about him that stood out in my mind...he'd moved in next door to me...I was dating another guy at the time...so Tom and I became friends. But the more we chilled together, the more obvious it became that there was something between us...I mean, we have everything in common and even though I cared about the guy I was with at the moment, it was nothing compared to the connection I had with Tom. So finally I broke up with my boyfriend, but Tom didn't know that it was because I had feelings for him. So Tom and I remained friends for two years and he went through many girlfriends and I was always the one he came to when things didn't work out...but I never told him how I felt about him.

It was our senior year now and I was asked to prom by this guy in my economics class. He was a nice guy but he wasn't who I really wanted to go with so I told him I already had a date. Then two weeks later three other guys asked me to prom, but still I said I already had a date, knowing that Tom probably wouldn't ask me cuz he'd been really quiet towards me lately, not his usual comfortable self. So I was pretty much planning on going with my best girl friends and just making the best of the evening.

One night I was lying in my bed about to fall asleep. I'd left my window open because it was really nice out. All of a sudden my favorite song, "The Rose," came on really faint. I didn't know where it was coming from so I got up and walked around my room and then looked out my window. From there, I could see directly into Tom's room, and he was looking out his window and I just stared at him for the longest time. Finally, he spoke, calling over between our lawns, "I've always loved you. Will you go to prom with me?"

I ran outside at the same time he did and when we met under the moon he picked me up and kissed me and I said, "What took you so long?" We're still together today and that was four years ago.

PROM NIGHT

Introduction

Prom night has slightly different meanings in Canada and the US. In Canada, prom night is always linked to graduation. It is preceded or followed by a cap and gown ceremony. Only seniors have a prom, and there is no junior prom. Although members of the lower grades may occasionally attend as dates, students typically go to only one prom during high school—their own. In Canada, prom night is more often called "grad," which makes the link with graduation and the end of high school fairly obvious.

In the US, on the other hand, prom night is not always linked to graduation. Senior prom clearly celebrates the end of high school and the transition into college or the workforce. But junior prom does not. Becoming a senior may confer a special status, yet the transition from junior to senior year is not as radical as the one which takes you right out of high school—it does not require celebration as such. In the US, moreover, people go to more than just their own proms: some girls may attend as many as four or five.

These are more than regional differences between the two countries. They are differences in the psychologies that fuel prom and prom night. Let's consider Canada first because the link between prom and graduation is so strong. To be leaving high school and entering the world of (young) adults is an intense experience. It comes with a sense of endings, especially in parts of Canada where there may be no junior and senior high—just a four or five year stretch in the same institution. It comes with uncertainty as you prepare for college (a new institution), or to enter the workforce (a new environment). And, it coincides with becoming of legal age for most things, including departure from the parental fold, marriage, and adult responsibility in general.

Because the moment of transition is so strong and occurs on so many levels, any event that coincides with this moment (the grad/prom party, in this case) becomes charged with the feelings characteristic of that moment. Psychologically, the grad/prom night party itself comes to symbolize the transition, containing within it (and releasing) the powerful feelings characteristic of this moment.

We find this happening with senior prom in the United States as well as Canada. As a party, or formal event, it is the focus for all the emotions one feels on ending high school and entering a (young) adult world. There is the same sense of finality, the pending dispersal of long-time friends, the uncertainty of a barely glimpsed future. Additionally, in both Canada and the US, there is the understanding on the parents' and educators' part, and in the culture in general, that prom night is a celebration of the end of high school and the beginning of a new stage in life. This understanding even allows parents and educators to condone behaviors on prom night they would find unacceptable at any other time.

But there is a still deeper psychological dimension to prom. Because of the link between the prom night party and graduation, this deeper dimension is not as clear in Canada as it is in the US. And in the US, it only becomes clear with the existence of junior prom: for junior prom is not about graduating, but about transforming crushes into couples. Senior prom is also about transforming crushes into couples; but because of its identification with graduation, this dimension is often obscured. Junior prom, on the other hand, has no other reason for being.

I make this crushes-to-couples claim based on two sets of evidence. First, the importance among juniors of selecting a partner and asking him or her formally to prom. One tends to select their crush first, friends second. One always asks formally, even if the moment of asking is not elaborately played out. Moreover, if one is going with a group of friends, or dateless, the understanding for many of them, especially at junior prom, is that this is a fallback measure and not the preferred way of attending prom—certainly not one's own prom. The second set of evidence concerns prom-goers' behavior on prom night and during the so-called after-prom: despite all the fun they are having, despite the craziness in the limos or on the dance floor, despite sharing dances with friends as well as one's date, or playing games or partying after prom, so many prom-goers spend the evening trying to hook up. The dance hall even sets the proper mood for hooking up. Prom themes are always romantic (and prom night is always themed). The decorations and lighting are romantic. Even the music is orchestrated so that there are more slow songs toward the end of the evening, giving potential couples more chances to come together as time runs out.

Last but not least, a few words about the stories included in this section. More than 85% of them address the crushes-to-couples process in one form or another, whether it is to mention it in passing or to make it the central topic. I did not intentionally choose stories that coincide with this theme; my selection reflects the prom night story submissions I have received over the years. If the submission ratios mirror what contributors are really thinking about when they think of prom, then graduating and moving on are not what concerns them most—it certainly doesn't concern them as juniors—although this is definitely present. Their big interest is hooking up; more specifically, becoming a couple with their crush, and doing so before time runs out—because after prom night, time has run out.

The Crushes-to-Couples Process

People who theorize about dramatic performances sometimes break down what happens onstage into two domains: setting and action. Setting is more than the stage space and how it's decorated. It also includes the events that take place within that space, which push and pull the characters this way and that. Action in turn, is not about words and behaviors. Action, as Aristotle said long ago, is a movement of spirit (in the character) toward completion, realization, transformation. The character experiences it at the level of the feelings. The action in Homer's *Odyssey*, for example, is Odysseus' struggle to get home again. As events (his setting) set him back or move him closer to his destination, so his feelings evolve, from expectation through frustration and anger, growing loneliness, doubt, and despair. When he arrives home, the action ends and his feelings are resolved—loneliness, doubt, anger, and frustration all turn to joy in his wife's embrace. This is the moment of resolution.

What does dramatic theory have to do with prom? Setting and action—prom is an identical structure. The prom night dance and after parties may be composed of glittering halls, ball gowns and tuxedos, fancy transportation, fine food, great music, sparkling conversation, smiles, laughter, dancing, and good times, but that is just the setting. True prom is what is happening at the level of the feelings, and the movement of spirit it embodies is the transformation from crush to couple, from two to one.

As you read the first story in this section, think about this process and imagine the narrator's feelings as the night progresses and he draws closer to his crush. The process that began when he asked the girl to be his prom date ends months later—as does prom—when he tells her how he feels and she returns the feelings. In dramatic terms, there is resolution.

Tim, HHS, GA (senior prom)

Well, this night was a much-anticipated one for me. It was my senior prom and I had asked this girl, Kristin (also a senior). She is a good friend of mine, but I'd never told her that I really like her. Well anyways, the day of prom we agreed that she would go over to Jennifer's place to get ready, and that I would then pick up Dale, who was Jennifer's date, and we would all meet at Jennifer's. The time came and I went to Dale's house.

It all happened as planned. We were running a bit late but it was no big deal. The girls were waiting for us when we arrived and when I saw Kristin, I couldn't believe my eyes. She was so beautiful that night, with her purple dress. My feelings for her instantly doubled! So we took some pictures at Jennifer's and then proceeded on to the Teen Advisor's house to take more pictures with a group of our friends. The Advisor's house was a nice place and we took pictures for what seemed like hours. My face was about to get a cramp from all that smiling, but it was fun.

The pictures done, the group broke up and Dale and his date and me and Kristin headed on to dinner, which is another adventure in itself. The restaurant was new, very nice though. We all ordered our meals, then when they arrived, about half of ours were screwed up, and one of the girls' salads had a rubber glove finger in it, so they gave us free desert, which was good. At that point I was thinking, great, what else can go wrong? So we left the restaurant and headed over to the prom dance. It was now about 10:30pm. We took more pictures and danced a little. It was fun, but the dance itself was not that big a deal.

After prom we all went over to our friend's house where we played games and watched movies. Everyone stayed up the whole night, then around 5:00 or 6:00am we all had some breakfast. Then some of us slept, others stayed up and talked. I went to bed, so did my date. I woke up about 9:00am, went home shortly after. But before I did, I talked with my date Kristin outside and told her how much of a great time I'd had with her. Then I told her how I felt about her and I asked her out. I also read her a poem I had written...she loved it! So now, a few weeks later, here we are...me and her are dating and having a great time with one another. It was an awesome night and I wish I could do it all over again.

Prom night, especially junior prom, produces more couples in a single night than are produced throughout the rest of the school year. Why is that? Because the essence of prom is the feelings toward another that prom-goers carry within them; and prom night provides the perfect stage for focusing those feelings and drawing them out into the open—thus transforming crushes into couples. If you missed this transformational process above, then consider the next story. It takes place in a different state on a different prom night in a different year, but it is the same story as the one you just read, creates the same overall mood, and finishes with the same alchemical transformation from crush to couple. Only the girl is telling it this time, and the names of the characters are different (and there's no salad incident)!

Mary, Orlando FL (junior prom)

I was sooo excited about prom! You know, the whole walking down the grand march when everyone looks at your gorgeous dress and then the dance and then the after-prom. I couldn't wait 'til grand march and the dance because I had the most gorgeous guy to go with and I was dying to dance with him. Well, the night came, and he picked me up in the limo he had rented. He looked incredible in his tux, even better than I had imagined. We walked in the grand march, and we waited 'til all of our friends walked through. Then the dance started at 9:00. I had liked my date for a long time, although I'd never told him my feelings, so that's why I was so excited to dance with him. We danced real close the entire time. It was great and I had the biggest grin on my face. And everybody could see it! All night he never left my side and he was the perfect gentleman. He even stood up from his chair every time I stood. But best of all, as the dance got closer to ending he wanted to dance even closer, so that my head was actually on his chest most of the time. It was incredible! Then the dance was over :(and it was time for after-prom :). They had so many fun games and people getting hypnotized. It was great. That got down at like 6:00 am. All of us decided that we should go out for breakfast because we were all kinda hungry, so we did. The whole time my guy stuck right next to me and we sat beside each other at the table and everything. And as we were going home from breakfast, he asked me out. The hunk I have like for three years had finally asked me out! I was sooo psyched! Of course I screamed YES!!!!! And now we've been together for almost a year and we're getting ready for our senior prom. We get to play the marvelous night all over again! :D

I can't resist. Here's another story that wonderfully articulates the expectation prom night creates, and that incredible moment when he or she says yes (not to mention that this story is beautifully written!).

Lovin guy, SHS, Los Angeles CA (senior prom)

My prom nite would be the most memorable nite of my life. My prom was held on the Queen Mary, a.k.a. "The Titanic," in Long Beach, California. The prom theme, which I came up with in the prom committee earlier that year, was "The Sea of Dreams." My prom was on a Thursday, but nobody seemed to mind, because as seniors, we didn't have to go to school the next day, which was called senior ditch day.

Well anyway, I had rented a brand new Mercedes Benz C230 sports coupe for two days, the day of prom, and after prom...it was really nice. So I went to pick up my date Vannessa, the most beautiful girl you will ever see. When she saw the car she was shocked and couldn't believe what she was going to ride in. But later on that night she would be even more surprised....

So we drove off to the Queen Mary, and once we set foot on the boat we felt like we were really on the Titanic and going to a ballroom dance. The hall was decorated beautifully, with smooth music playing...just the right mood for a special surprise for my date. We sat at our table and ate a very delicious Italian dish. After we were done eating we went to take pictures. After we were done taking pictures and eating, the dance started and we went up to dance. We were having the best time. We danced an hour and a half non-stop before we decided to rest our feet for a little while.

We sat and talked a bit and then I asked Vannessa if she would like to take a walk to see the view of downtown Long Beach from the boat, and she said she would love to. So we walked around the Queen Mary. It was a very long walk, so we stopped where they filmed the famous scene where Rose was standing up on the balcony with Jack and she tells him she's flying. Well anyway, we were standing at the very same spot when I took out a rose that I had hidden in my coat pocket... luckily the rose was still in perfect condition. I gave her the rose, then I took out a piece of paper where I had written a poem for her, and I read it. I was so nervous, thinking in my head, "I can't believe I'm doing this, I hope she says yes."

In the poem I asked Vannessa to be my girlfriend. So after I read the poem, I told her how I felt about her and asked her the question directly, "Would you do me the honor of being my girlfriend?" And she agreed! I was so happy! I gave her a big hug and kissed her, under the stars and moonlight. It was our first kiss.

We then went back inside to dance our first slow dance as a couple. The song was "Never Had a Dream Come True" by S Club 7, followed by "All My Life" by K-Ci & JoJo. What more perfect songs to dance to than these!

After prom was over, we went cruising along with my best friend and his girlfriend in the Mercedes that I had rented. First, we went to Hollywood, and then to Santa Monica Beach to see the sunrise. Then we went to eat breakfast at a restaurant, and at last to Vannessa's house. I slept over because her mom was a little scared that something would happen to me because I hadn't slept all night, and so I agreed, and I slept on the floor next to her bed...no I did not sleep with her.

So that was my prom night, and as you can see, it will always be a memorable night for me and her.

In the next story we see a small evolution from the preceding three stories. What happens is, he does not get the girl (sorry about giving away the ending). But what's important if we are to understand prom night is that not getting the girl in this case proves that prom is all about getting the girl (or guy)—that it's about hooking up. Of course, you have to pay special attention to his feelings—the expectation, the desire, and the letdown because these are where the story, the drama, is really happening.

A True Gent, Fairfield CA (junior prom)

"A NIGHT AT THE OSCARS" was the theme of our prom. It was held at the San Francisco City Hall on a Saturday. The prom was mixed, juniors and seniors, this being my junior prom.

I had the perfect tux to go with the perfect girl. All right, let me give you people some background. When first I asked my date to go with me to my junior prom, I told her that I didn't want to go with her if she had a man. So! Everything was going great until the moment she told me she had a boyfriend. That moment was prom night, after I'd already come to pick her up, before leaving to dinner.

If you readers think that this story goes downhill from here, you're wrong...because we still had fun...don't think "dirty...".

She was wearing a very beautiful dark royal blue dress with her hair up and blue flowers in her hair, with her body smelling hella GOOD...If you're wondering, I love it when girls show off their neck...and their hair is all up. I must have told her that she looked beautiful like a million times. And I don't lie; I just call them as they come.

I tried my hardest to respect her as a taken woman. I was upset with her for not telling me beforehand, because I had this day all planned out for the two of us...If you're wondering, Yes! I do like this girl.

Anyhow, we left to dinner, and "DINNER WAS OFF THE HOOK"...We both ate pasta and choped it up...After dinner we went to take some pics by the bay, it was kewl....

After that we went to City Hall for the dance. I'm not gonna lie...YES! We did get freaky on the dance floor...Who doesn't? The drinks were good, went down smooth and slow. With us looking so fine together, it sucked telling people, "NO" when they asked, "Do you guys go out?...Man...Oh well...I had hella fun with her, laughing and dancing, looking into her incredible eyes as we slow danced.

If it wasn't for her having a boyfriend, I could have been taken by now. If only she knew how much I cared for her! Ever since we kissed hella days ago, at the start of junior year, at a party, I was hooked. Thinking I could hook up with her as a couple at prom was one of the reasons why I asked her to go with me (is that wrong?).

There was this moment we had that didn't go so well. It was just us two at this table, being very quiet and not talking...when suddenly I realized, that for my senior prom, no way I'm going with a friend, I gotta have a girlfriend by then. The night's too magical not to be hooked up or to hook up. I felt sad that moment, even though I was surrounded by the beauty of the night and by my date's...untouch-able...beauty.

Anyways, we got back on the dance floor, 'cause that's where we had the most fun. Then when the DJ said, "LAST SONG, COUPLES ONLY," we both looked at each other and stayed on the dance floor. The song was "Tender Love." I'm not gonna ever forget that moment...She locked her hands around my neck and I placed my hands gently on her hips and we began to dance, nice and slow. I had so many feelings running through me, I felt like kissing her neck, but I couldn't...Because of her freakin' boyfriend, I had to respect her...So! I got myself under control and blanked out my mind and just went with the flow.

That was pretty much it... :(... Our ride picked us up and on the way back she fell asleep in my arms with "Tender Love" playing on the slow jams CD I'd made.

If I had to say what my favorite part of the day was, I would say it was when I saw her for the first time in her dress, when I picked her up. I have that moment pictured in my mind FOREVER....

A Marriage Connection

At first I thought this next story had to be a bogus submission, because the names in it are all so weird. Who calls their son Boston, and their twin daughters Paris and London? It didn't help, either, that Paris's boyfriend was called Landon. A few sentences into the story, and my head was spinning. Still, the story Paris tells is quite beautiful—and no, it is not bogus. The tie-in between prom and marriage (you'll see it below), is particularly important because it points out just how meaningful prom is: it's the sort of event one mentions in the same breath as marriage; and that means that, unconsciously or not, one is often thinking of it on the same level.

Paris, Elk Grove CA (senior prom)
Gosh, where do I start? At first I didn't really plan on going to senior prom 'cause I had never gone to any of the other dances. I had been asked, but I just never did. Well, I finally got talked into it and asked my boyfriend Landon to go. Of course he said yes! So we started making plans. I didn't have a clue where to start so he kinda took over. We planned to go with my brother, Boston, who is eighteen, his date, and my twin sister, London. And since she didn't have a date, we hooked her up with Travis (my boyfriend's best friend). Like every other girl, London and I had to look for the perfect dresses. We searched high and low. We also couldn't decide if we wanted to go as matching twins or not. So finally...one month before prom, we were in Hawaii, and we found the dresses. We are both perfect size 4s, with long gold blonde hair that goes down past our butts (we haven't cut it in ten years), and hazel eyes. We found strapless, long, mint green dresses. They were fitted at the top, with tons of little diamonds clustered all over that rained down the front of the dresses. They were gorgeous! We did our own hair since we didn't trust anyone else to do it. We did it kinda half up and down, with little diamonds all over the front of our hair. We looked like we had walked out of a fairy tale. Boston's

girlfriend (who happens to be my best friend, Krystle) wore an ice pink dress that shimmered.

The guys planned the whole prom, but they kept everything secret from us. They said that all we had to do was make ourselves look beautiful, so that's what we did. So prom night came and we had just finished the last touches when the doorbell rang. My mom answered the door and let the gentlemen in. Us three girls slowly made our appearance. We were a sight to see and so were they!! My boyfriend looked drop-dead gorgeous in his tux. He and Travis had matching tuxes to match my sister and me, who had gone as matching twins after all, and Boston matched Krys. They bought us the most beautiful corsages I had ever seen! After like a thousand pictures we finally went outside. They had a new black Hummer limo waiting for us!! Man, were we surprised!! We went to this really nice and expensive restaurant for dinner in Old Sac, then walked by the river 'til it was time to go to the dance. We had it at the gym, and it looked wonderful!! So we danced almost every dance, then us girls went to the restroom real quick and when we came out we couldn't find our dates anywhere!!! We looked for like ten minutes and everyone had like a funny look on their faces when we asked if they had seen them! Then all of a sudden…there they were! On stage, and each of them said something special about each of us. Then they sang "Back at One," by Brian McKnight. We all started to cry. Then they came and danced the last dance with us. When it was over, Landon gave me the sweetest kiss he had ever given me. And that still wasn't the end of the night.

Instead of the usual after-prom get together, they took us in the limo to San Francisco!! We walked the pier at three in the morning with no one there but us three couples! It was the best night of my life (Travis and London are now going out, too!!!).

I hope your prom was as great as mine. And for those of you that have yet to experience it, remember, girls, this is your night and not every guy is as sweet as mine and the other two. Don't do anything you will regret. Your prom night is a night for memories, whether good or bad, you will decide. It has been almost a year and we are all still together. Boston and Krystle will be married this summer, and Landon and I this fall. London and Travis will be married at Christmas. For some, prom is just another night to store away with special memories. For others (me!) it was the start of a fairy tale dream come true.

Prom and marriage both share the same emotional intensity we reserve for the more meaningful moments in our lives. Both, likewise, are about the formation of couples. On prom night, especially junior prom, most crushes move up a level and become boyfriends or girlfriends for the first time. If that bond that was established prom night holds, then they may move up yet another level, into marriage, as did London, Paris, and Krystle. But what about those people who go to prom and are already boyfriend and girlfriend, especially if they have been together for a long time? Well, sometimes they openly and publicly make the connection between prom and marriage—it is not unusual for a boyfriend to propose to his girlfriend on prom night.

Amanda, Forsyth High School, Forsyth MO (senior prom)

Our prom was perfect, couldn't ask for more, couldn't ask for less. I went with Josh, my boyfriend of two years…everyone used to say we would eventually end up together. Our theme was "A Night To Remember," which it definitely was! So me and Josh were dancing the night away and having a great time. A very upbeat song came on and we were screaming and dancing all over the place. Then all of a sudden a slow song, our theme song in fact, came on, and we were all slow dancing. At one point during the song, I noticed that somehow we'd gotten to the middle of the floor. Everyone had pushed away from us and a spotlight was on me and Josh. If I haven't mentioned it, then don't forget that I hate that kind of attention. I was like, what's going on? when the music got real quiet, and Josh got down on one knee. I still didn't get it. What was Josh doing? I was like, are you ok, get up. And he looked up at me, squeezed my hands and said, "Amanda L_____, will you marry me?" I almost choked. I had no idea he was going to ask me. My eyes were filling with tears. I said yes and gave a tug on him and he stood up and we made out through the rest of the song while everyone clapped and cheered.

But…the night didn't end like every other prom. We went back to my house to change and stuff, and…I didn't know about any of this…his family and my family were all together in the living room, and when we walked in everyone was like, "SURPRISE!" It was really awesome. Everyone but me knew about it. And now that college is starting and we are living in an apartment on campus, we have decided to get married on his birthday, which is in September. I am really looking forward to it!

Dark Fairy-Tale Prom

Not all stories end well, or with romance and hooking up. Sometimes the opposite happens, and a fairy-tale night transforms into a dark fairy tale—where there was romance and hooking up, now there is loss and breaking up. The next four stories are all about hookings-up that went wrong, or about expectations that weren't met, and the distress this produces. In some of these stories the characters are attempting the transformation from crush to couple, but someone or something gets in the way of completing the process. In others, the characters used to go out but broke up before prom. When they meet again on prom night, they realize their true feelings for each other—but the realization comes too late.

Rachael, Summerville SC (senior prom)

My prom was yesterday. Here's my story, but you'll have to understand the circumstances to know why I felt the way I did prom night and still feel today. Me and my long-time boyfriend broke up about a month before prom. We had already decided to go together so we thought we would just stick with the plan. We had one of those big dramatic breakups, but luckily no one was around to see it. We had even been engaged. The problem was that I wasn't sure if he was really the one for me. I knew I loved him, but I just wasn't sure if it was the kind of love that would last forever. I finally dumped him because I thought he was cheating on me (he wasn't, but I guess I still wanted to break up, and I used that as an excuse). Well he came over about two days later and asked me back out. I thought about it, and said yes. That weekend I went over to his house and he said he wasn't sure about us getting married, but that he knew he loved me—he just didn't know if I was the one. I told him that I didn't want him to lead me on, so we should just break up. He agreed, and we broke up for the second and last time.

That was more than a month ago, and today—yesterday—I found

out I really did love him. I wouldn't know that 'til prom night. I didn't know what I had until it was gone, and it was gone for good.

He came over to my house the day of prom. I always told him that he looked like Val Kilmer from *Batman Beyond,* and in his tux he looked even more like him. My focus was completely on him and I didn't care about anything else. Somehow, as he came through my front door, I knew I was lost without him and I wanted to spend the rest of my life with him. We went to prom. The hall was so romantic...the theme was, "A Red Carpet Affair." I waited all night for him to tell me he loved me and that he missed me. I didn't know if that was how he felt, but I felt that way and I wanted him to also feel like that. We held hands most of the time and he held me the way he used to when we were together...it made me miss him so much.

The night flew by and the last song was Whitney Houston's "I Will Always Love You." He kissed me during the whole song and it played forever. Believe me, girls, when you're kissed by the man you love...there could be thousands of people in the room and he's the only one you can see. We snuggled up close on the way home. He told me how beautiful I was and I wanted to tell him how much I loved him, but I couldn't. He walked me to my door and hugged me. I went to reach for the doorknob and he grabbed my hand and kissed me like he really meant it. He put his forehead on mine so our noses were touching and said, "our very last kiss."

I went to bed last night with a broken heart. We didn't get back together. I loved him too late. I let the man of my dreams get away. To my Batman, if you ever read this, "I will always love you."

☆ ☆ ☆ ☆ ☆

So did you cry as you read the last story? Because if you did, then you're getting very close to understanding the power and the beauty of prom night. It lies in the intensity of the feelings it evokes. But it does more than that. For example, it can change the very way we feel about a person. Prom night is, among other things, a kind of stage on which you prove yourself to your date. Based on your performance that evening, your date will judge whether it's worth hooking up with you or not—either they will cool toward you or they will move toward you. The following story, a sad one, beautifully illustrates this, and how the wrong move, or the wrong attitude, can forever change the way your once potential partner will see you.

Anita, San Diego CA (senior prom)

It was my senior prom and I was very excited for it. I'd had a crush on this guy for about a year and I could only think of going to prom with him. The only downfall to this plan was that he barely knew I was alive. I turned down several other guys because he was the only person I wanted to go with, and before I knew it, it was a week before prom and I was dateless. Somehow, I got the majority of my friends to tell him to ask me, and amazingly it happened. I couldn't stop smiling for that entire week. Anyways, we went to prom with a huge group of friends, and later most everybody agreed we were the cutest couple in the group. Well we arrive at prom, it's at a dumb place, a hotel, and he has not yet hugged me, held my hand or anything. Actually, it turns out the closest we got the entire night was when he placed the corsage on my wrist. But let's jump forward in time, shall we? It's the last song of the night, and all I want is one dance because I hadn't even danced with anybody else because I wanted to dance with my date. It took me a while to find him, but I finally saw him looking from the sidelines watching all the couples dance. I said, "Would you like to dance?" and he replied, "No, not really. I don't dance." It was useless, so I said all right, and pretended not to care as he walked from the ballroom into another room. I sat down at a table with several other girls who were either dateless or who were incapable of dancing because of a broken limb. I just sat there and cried. I told no one, and just sat there.

We finished up the night together, but we were awkward around each other now. Without my saying it, he knew I was really bummed about the evening. The awkwardness remained in the coming weeks and we barely spoke to each other again. It was only several weeks later that my date finally said he was sorry that he didn't dance, and hoped I understood. I did and I do. But unhappily, that changed things between us, and although I still like him, somehow I can't see us together anymore :(.

Prom night operates like a stage to focus and intensify feelings—all feelings. When you hook up with your crush and become a couple, the feelings are powerful, yet they are joyful, happy. When the hook-up goes wrong, the feelings are just as powerful, but they are sorrowful, sad. In the next story, Andres, the narrator, goes through the prom night process that transforms crushes into couples—but he does so alone, because his date does not return his feelings. If you read closely enough, you can glimpse "what should have been" filtering out through the cracks in "what is"—like a script that has been poorly edited.

Andres, Wethersfield CT (junior prom)

What can I say? I didn't know what to expect. The girl who I asked to the prom I considered the kindest, sweetest, most beautiful girl I had ever met. She was the only one I wanted to ask, and she accepted. The two of us were very good friends in school. But there was something about her that made her special. She never showed a weakness inside her and smiled a smile that could brighten the darkest day. She was the only girl that really talked to me for more than just a few seconds and she always sat next to me. I believe that she saw me as who I was, and not just a shy boy who stutters. So when she accepted my offer I was thrilled.

A couple of weeks later, the tides changed. On a weekend band trip she started to get close to a guy she is really good friends with and they started to go out. Even though I shouldn't have, I felt devastated and heartbroken. I talked to her about it and she still wanted to go to the prom with me. That puzzled me, but I accepted. I still felt depressed because I knew that even by the time that night was over and all the magic of the evening spent, I would still mean nothing to her.

As prom approached, I could kind of sense that she wasn't excited. She didn't want to buy pictures or stay at the party afterwards. On prom night, the first time I saw her was a heart-melting experience. She was more beautiful than anything I could ever imagine. But still I could sense her lack of desire to come. On the limo ride there, she didn't really either talk to me or look at me. At dinner, her "boyfriend" somehow came up in the conversation. But it was when we danced that I had to tell her my feelings. When we were slow dancing to Louis Armstrong's "What a Wonderful World," I whispered in her ear that she was the most beautiful girl I had ever seen. There was a long pause, and then she said, "Thank you." I didn't know if I had made her uncomfortable or not, but I told her I meant it from the bottom of my heart. After the last song, just as I was about to pull away, she gave me a big hug.

The limo ride home was about the same, without much eye contact. But it was the moment when the limo dropped her off at her house that I remember best. She gave me a hug like no other and said, "Thank you so much, I had a wonderful time." I then proceeded to tell her it was one of the happiest days of my life, and then I kissed her on the cheek. All of this just happened two days ago, so I haven't seen her yet. I hope I haven't made her uncomfortable. I meant everything I said from the bottom of my heart. She probably won't break up with her boyfriend and her senior prom with him will be more memorable to her. That gives me a great deal of pain, but I've got to let her do the thing that will make her happy. I would do anything to win her heart. That night was truly a night I will always remember. Hopefully, she will too.

I'd say the narrator in the next story has a bit of an attitude. But she's a heck of a writer, even if she doesn't think so; and her story is long, complex, and ultimately, sad. The story also provides a very good illustration of the power prom night has over those of us who still have proms to attend. This girl clearly does not want to go; nor does she think much of prom—"a stupid dance thing" she calls it. And yet she goes. And when she does, the forces that govern prom sweep her up just as they do anyone else. She does not hook up with her ex—it's too late for that—but prom night brings them closer together again, if only for a short while, even as it makes her realize her true feelings for him.

Anonymous, Fort Smith AR (junior prom)

Here in Arkansas, prom is known to some as a stupid dance thing and
for others it is a special moment/night. I, well, I did not give a damn
about prom and was among those who thought it was a stupid thing.
Prom, I thought, comes and goes, so here was my junior prom and I
might as well go! My friend had been asked to junior prom and she
said she turned him down because it wasn't her senior year and it had
to be special and so on.

I didn't care how special it is. Prom was prom. I was asked the
first week of school to go to prom. First I said yes, and months later I
refused. I just didn't want to go through the trouble of finding a dress
and all that. My now-ex-date's friend offered to buy my dress if I'd go
with his friend, but still I refused. Later in the school year, all my
junior friends were invited and they accepted. They begged me so
desperately to go that I finally gave in. But right when I decided to go,
everyone who had asked me to prom had already found a date. So
instead of trying to get out of going to prom, now I was trying to get
in! This guy told me that this other guy was selling his ticket because
he broke up with his girlfriend. So I bought it. He wasn't my date,
and thankfully he wasn't! I felt weird not having a date, so my friends
hooked me up with someone. I didn't dislike him but I just couldn't
stand him. I swear, I tried everything to be nice to him, but I couldn't
help it, I lost my patience and finally ditched him later during prom.

Well, let's talk about before-prom first. I woke up around 7 and
left around 9 to go decorate the prom. My friends picked me up at
10:30 to go do my hair. It started raining and we had to go to Wal-
Mart to buy powder because I had left mine at school. Then we had to
go all the way to Wal-Mart Supercenter because I needed a bigger bra.
LOL. Yeah, I said it. My dress was a perfect fit but the breast part was
too extended for a girl with little stuff. So after that we traveled back
to little Wal-Mart to get some more things we'd forgotten. It was still
raining. Then we went to my friend's house, where she did me and my
friend's make-up.

When we were done, we had to go by a friend's house to get her
prom dress. Guess what? Her door was locked and she had the wrong
key. So we went into her backyard, where her wild dog runs off as
soon as she opens the fence gate. They chased him for about 15 minutes. I had my dress on so I stood on the porch going "o...m...g.,"

banging my forehead on the door. So when they finally got the dog, my friend tried climbing up the window but it was too high. So we dragged this big heavy barrel that took us another 15 minutes to get to the window. My friend used it and made her way into her house.

After that we went to my friend's date's house where my date picked me up. He took me to my other friend's house where everyone was at. Well to make it short and less confusing, we went to the Lighthouse restaurant and ate. The food sucked. Then we all went to the prom together. Short enough?

Sooo...the prom was held at Holiday Inn, in the ballroom. We had to go through this room full of beautiful plants and several water-falls. It was a perfect entrance. The very moment we got into prom, we ran onto the dance floor while they were doing the cha cha. The room wasn't as bad as I thought. The theme was "A Midsummer Night's Dream." There were pretty but fake waterfalls, water springs, and the place was covered in beautiful flowers.

So yeah, like I said above, I ended up ditching my date. I felt bad but then it actually didn't turn out that bad leaving him, because everyone in my group also left their dates. No one really gave a care. Everyone was having a good time. While getting a drink of water, I saw my ex passing by. I yelled his name and gave him a hug. I was actually surprised I acted. My ex and I broke up almost a year ago. We were best friends for a year and then we decided to hook it up. It was a very depressing period after the break up. He's a senior and we always planned to go to the prom together. It didn't happen. As time went on, we started to dislike each other. We misunderstood each other and what made us hate each other more was other people, who came between us and talked bad to each of us about the other...and we chose to believe it. He started dating another girl several months after we broke up and I've been off and on with guys. My feelings for him still remained, though, and after prom night, the feelings were too strong for me to hide. You could say, through the year, we've acted as if we hated each other but we didn't. It was so hard to cope without him. Slowly, as the year came to an end, we started to get closer. Prom was where we began to talk more.

So after the hug we stood there and talked a bit. I asked him why he wasn't dancing, and he said the song playing sucked bootie. Yeah, he was right, it did. Then he asked me to chill here until they played a

good song. Jay-Z's "Can I Get A..." came on, so I took him out to the
dance floor and we started dancing. Woot woot. It was great to have
him close again. After the song, we went off the stage and saw glow
sticks being passed out so we went after them. He followed me and I
wrapped my arm around his. There were his silly friends throwing out
some words like, "ooh pimp!" or "you tight!" and stuff like
"daaaaaaaaaaaamn." People at my school said we would make a gorgeous couple. They didn't know we used to go out. Well we got our
glow sticks and headed back onto the stage floor. A slow song came
on, Daniel Bedingfield's "If You're Not the One." We paused a bit
and then we danced. I was happy. It was actually a moment I'd never
thought would happen with him. After all we've been through, things
that people wouldn't understand but have talked about anyway, that
moment with him was "my special moment." That moment, I felt like
I was in the spotlight for some reason. It seemed as if everyone on
that dance floor was smiling at us. Well actually they did. =P
Everybody seemed happy that we were close. I was more than happy.

After that, he told me to follow him and so I did. He walked me
over and pulled up a chair for me to sit. There he introduced me to
his date and I greeted her. She mad-dogged me, actually. I looked at
my ex and we both just shrugged. We talked for a bit, then he told me
he had to go to the restroom. I told him okay and that I'd be over
there with my friends. From time to time he would drop by to see how
I was doing. Prom ended and off to after-prom everybody went. It was
held at Bowling World. There I spotted him and we chatted. It was
only 2am but I was beat, so I went home. After-prom usually ends
around 6am.

Well, that was my night. It wasn't as mushy and romantic as you
might expect. But that night with him was everything to me. It was my
unexpected dream that I had wished for, to share my night with him.
From that moment on, the thought of it remains in my dreams and
I'm sure it'll probably be there for a while. I realized that after a year
of chaos and hatred, he has never once left my heart.

Prom was May 24th. Today is May 29th. Tomorrow, he's graduating. Right now, I don't know what to say about it. But I can surely go
on about our past. I am happy and blessed to have shared that night
with him. It is sad that it took us a year to come together as close
friends again. I regret so many things, mostly all that wasted time,

because right when things were getting better, it is time for him to part. It's so hard to lose the one you love.

Maurice, you will always be in my heart despite everything. I will never forget you. You showed me more than the meaning of life; you showed me the feeling of love. If there were one wish I could grant here tonight, it would be to have you back by my side. Maurice, through it all, I've never stopped thinking of you. You were always there in my mind and heart. Thank you for the precious feelings you have delivered to my heart. ^-^

So yeah, that's my story. I hope it wasn't too mushy or dull, and please excuse my writing. I am very bad at writing and explaining. Words can never express everything for me. You just had to be there. I wrote a short poem for him; you can read it below if you like. Thanks for reading this far!

This was the day I've been waiting for to come
We split for a year and now we're back as one
When you left I was still able to see you, but now we part
Finally I realize that you have never once left my heart
I won't be able to see you as I used to
But now I know that you'll always be there
You'll be far away but you remain
Around me, in my heart, and everywhere
You live forever in my mind
You're a piece of my world, my source of life,
You're my air.

Friendship

Now we come to a shift in the nature of prom as we have discussed it previously. So that you do not start to believe prom night is exclusively for the formation (or breakup) of couples, the next six stories have friendship as the guiding theme, not budding love. In this next story, the narrator insists that "having a date isn't so important...having a good time, with good friends, is what matters." She may be right—it's not for me to say. When I read her story, though, it sounds wistful when she says she did not have a date to her senior prom. And when she says that she in a sense ended up with three dates, all of them her friends, it sounds—to me—suspiciously like a fallback measure.

Nicole, Hayfield Secondary, Alexandria VA (senior prom)

I've been reading all these gorgeous stories about proms that were saved from the brink of disaster...and I just had to add my story to the pile. Not all happy endings are filled with partners reuniting or roses and candles with notes about unconfessed secret crushes.

In 1996 my school was blazing with excitement over our senior prom, the only prom I ever attended. I know you're thinking LOSER! right now, but wait! The story gets better. So everyone is enveloped in conversation about dresses, shoes, tuxes, fancy dinners, alcohol, and of course, DATES. I'm sure you can guess by now that I was dateless. Oh, not hopeful, not having a friend that would come to the rescue...I was completely dateless. To make things even worse, I was living with my best friend's family because my mom was in the process of separating from her abusive/alcoholic husband. Yay. My state of mind was not the best...but I resolved that SOMEHOW, I would make it to that prom. It was the only senior prom I'd have...the only one that really mattered to me. Date or not, I was determined to go.

One day, my wicked stepfather showed up at the door where I was staying, and handed me an envelope with $200 in it. That was the most money I had ever seen at that point in my life. I am eternally grateful to him for that…it is the one thing he ever gave me without strings attached. I thanked him, and then made that $200 really count. I got a dress, shoes, chipped in with some pals for a limo, and I even had money left over for dinner. I went to prom with the best guys in the whole world. It was three couples, and then me.

My chubby thighs were concealed, but my nonexistent bust was not. :o> My makeup wasn't great, and my hair was incredibly frizzy, but somehow, I managed to pose for pictures and fake a smile. I arrived last at my buddy Marcus' house, but that was okay, because the limo was an hour and a half late!! When I got there, they had a corsage…for me. The rest of the night, all three guys proceeded to take extra good care of me. Richard helped me out of the limo, and Drew pulled out my chair at dinner. So I guess you could say that I ended up with three dates! Those boys made me feel like a queen.

Prom was special, and it was worth the struggle to get there. Keep your heads up, girls. Having a date isn't so important… having a good time, with good friends, is what matters.

This next story is about good friends—no, great friends. Although it is about friends, the crush-to-couple theme is prominent. Even the connection with marriage is made. However, the story is very, very sad. I won't say more but just let you read it.

Bradley, SDHS, San Diego, CA (senior prom)

My friend Jody had been going out with this really good-looking guy named Trent. They were like the Dream Couple. She was cheerleader and he was quarterback. They were the most popular couple at our school. About three months before our senior prom, Jody was diagnosed with cancer. She was devastated when her beautiful, dark brown hair started falling out. She was even more devastated when the "perfect" boyfriend dumped her the week before prom. Trent and I never really got along (Trent=Prep, I=Punk). Nearly all of her hair had fallen out by prom day and she had been reduced to wearing a wig. We used to joke about how at least she could have whatever hair color she wanted now. She had picked out her prom dress like the first day of school.

I decided that I was going to ask her to go to the prom with me since we were the BEST of friends, so I went over to her house early that day to put my plan into action. Her mom answered the door and was very shocked at my appearance. My hair was very neatly trimmed (until then, I'd had the biggest Mohawk throughout high school) and I was holding a small box. She enveloped me in a hug and told me that Jody was upstairs in her room and had been in there all day crying. I walked up the stairs as quietly as I could and peeked around the corner into her room. She was lying on her bed looking at a picture of her and Trent at the park. I knocked on her door gently. She told me to come in and I went in and sat down on the edge of her bed.

She asked me why I wasn't getting ready for prom and I handed her the box. Inside was a diamond-studded silver choker with a matching bracelet. She threw her arms around me and sobbed for about 30 minutes. When she was done she looked up and told me that this was the sweetest thing anyone had ever done for her. I gave her a big hug and kissed her gently on the cheek and told her that if we were going, then we'd have to get ready. I left her house and went home and got my tux on and grabbed her next surprise, as well as her corsage, and rushed back to her house.

Prom would be starting soon. I knocked on her front door and her mom answered, then called up the stairs to Jody. When Jody rounded the corner I thought I was going to faint. It was the most beautiful thing I had ever seen. She was wearing the wig that looked SO much like her natural hair and her dress was navy blue. She descended the stairs like an angel. When she finally got down, I pinned her corsage on her and then her mom did the usual parent thing: pre-prom pictures and all that.

We at last started off to the prom, where we had the time of our lives. Her friends had nominated her for prom queen and she of course was crowned. When the last dance came around I led her out to the dance floor. When the dance was over I pulled a small box (her next surprise) out of my pocket and got down on one knee. She looked so confused until I began to speak. This is what I said: "Jody, you are the most beautiful girl here tonight. I couldn't have asked God for a more perfect night. I love you with all of my heart and soul." I opened the box to reveal a diamond engagement ring. "Jody H____, will you marry me?" She then began crying uncontrollably as I slipped the ring on her finger. She didn't have to say yes. I could feel her answer.

We never actually got married because a month before the date we set her cancer won the battle. She's been gone for six years. We both knew that we would never legally be man and wife, but we loved each other all the same. Jody, I love you so much! Wait for me. I pray to be there soon.

The first story in this Friendship chapter hinted that going with a friend is fine, but that it is still a fallback measure, no matter how well you disguise it. One usually prefers a date over a friend, especially for one's senior prom. This next story is about great friends, not crushes (and it should lighten the mood a bit). Yes, going with a friend is a fallback measure in this narrative, too. But what a fallback measure! Because these two make it look like they're going out in every way that counts—and you'd never know it was a perfect act. Finally, bear in mind as you read: envy and revenge are a type of feeling.

Lisa, Ann Arbor, MI (senior prom)

I was taught that you should forgive those who hurt you. I was also taught that envy is one of the cardinal sins. But what about the envy of others when it's directed at you? Is it a sin if you take a secret pleasure in other people's envy of you? Because in many ways, that's what my prom was all about!

So my story starts. It was the beginning of senior year and that summer my family moved us across the city, which meant I had to transfer schools. I was really bummed because senior year is supposed to be the best. But all my friends, and all the people I grew up with, were no longer at my school. Instead, here were all these new faces, and not always the kindest or friendliest ones. The people in general—but especially the girls—in my year were really snobby and cliquey. No matter how I tried—and I tried, believe me!—they wouldn't let me into their circle. I tried dressing as they did, because it seemed that looks were everything to them. I tried interesting myself in the things that rocked their world, whether it was the guys they were into, or their music, their endless shopping, or non-stop chatter about how it must suck to be other people. But nothing helped and eventually I gave up. My personality just didn't fit with theirs. My looks, even in expensive brand-name clothes, remained too mousy.

By January, that was all behind me, and I was wondering why I'd bothered trying to make friends in the first place. Lonely or not at this new school, my time here was almost up and college was coming. So as they say, best to suck it up and keep moving. I was pretty quiet to begin with, but now I really clammed up and kept strictly to myself. Unfortunately, instead of letting me become invisible, all those people I'd originally tried to make friends with started teasing me. They teased me because I didn't have any friends. They teased me because I was so quiet. Since prom was fast approaching, they assumed that I would never find a prom date, and they teased me about that too.

Mousy, miserable me felt pretty sure they were right.

Well, two weeks before prom, my best friend, Erik, and I were talking, and I was telling him my tale of woe. Erik has been my best friend since I was about five. He's still my best friend today. We went out for a year when we were sixteen, but it didn't feel right, and after we broke it up he told me he was gay. Since then, we've been closer than ever, and there's nothing we don't share, nothing we wouldn't do for each other. The other thing about Erik is that he's easily the hottest guy I've ever seen other than on TV.

So, we talked my prom dilemma over and he said he would be my prom date. I thought it would be great to have my friend escort me, but I was also wishing that I could show my new classmates a thing or two, if only to prove that I was neither so friendless nor so unable to get a hott date for prom, especially if it involved romance. However, I never mentioned this wish to Erik, and I even felt guilty for having it—after all, we should forgive and forget, which is what I've always been taught. It would have felt good to show those people up, though....

Prom night arrived at last and Erik and I were driving to the dance. He'd rented a vintage Corvette for us, he was wearing this amazing tux and he looked more gorgeous than ever. We were just nearing the hotel where prom was to be held when he turned to me

and said, "Just for tonight, I'm gonna go back into the closet."
Although I had my suspicions, I asked him what he meant anyway, and
he replied, "We're going to make every single person at your prom
green with envy, just wait and see."

We reached the hotel and let the valet park our car. Some of the
girls were outside with their dates, hanging around the door waiting
to see other couples arrive. I could see them looking Erik and me up
and down, and I could tell by the look in their eyes that they couldn't
believe I was here at prom with someone like him. So the first thing
he did was right there, before we even got up the stairs, he held me by
the waist and gave me a light kiss on the lips, as if it were the most
natural thing in the world, something we'd been doing for years. I
couldn't help but smile, and in surprise, I kissed him right back.
Then he took my hand and we went up the stairs and passed inside,
and he didn't even glance at the other girls standing around, although
they looked incredible in their gowns and updos.

The rest of the night he was all clingy. He wouldn't leave my side.
He danced all the slow songs with me and kissed me and held me close
as we danced. When other girls asked him to dance, he would always
say thanks but no, that he was here with me! He was simply amazing,
because he made it appear as if he and I had been going out forever.
Everyone was so surprised that mousy, quiet little me had such a
charming "boyfriend."

We had a wonderful night. It's a year later now, and I'm still single
(sigh). But I'm having a great time at college, and I'm much more
confident about myself, especially because I'm in an environment
where the cliques haven't had time to form yet—and where it probably
won't matter if they do. Yes, Erik and I are still best friends, although
he attends a different college. As for prom night, it was a wonderful
night. I know I didn't have the typically ideal prom, but you know, I
spent it with my closest friend, and I was so touched by what he did
for me that I think I was happier that night than anyone else there.

And the envy thing? Yeah, it felt good. What can I say…forgive
and forget, but get yours first!

Sacrifices friends wouldn't ordinarily make on any other night, they gladly make on prom night—including flying a thousand miles so their friend won't go to prom dateless. In this story, there is no hooking up, and there is no intention of hooking up; it is strictly between friends. Note, though, that Keri would have preferred a date to her friend—except that nobody asked her.

Keri, PHS, Plattsburgh NY (senior prom)

Well, it was finally time for my senior prom. I had always said that I would never go, and up until about a week before prom, I still didn't want to go. I had a strong feeling that no one would ever ask me, but I got my dress and everything anyway. I really didn't want to go alone, so I called my best friend, Jason, who lives in North Carolina (I live in New York). I told him that I really missed him and asked him if he would come up and go to prom with me. He said he'd love to and thought it would be a lot of fun, considering we hadn't seen each other in two years. This was about six months before prom, when I had already gotten all fatal about it. Then, about two months later he started dating this girl. Everything changed and we didn't talk as much anymore. I asked him again about prom and he said that he couldn't come now. When I asked him why, he said that his girlfriend didn't want him to go because she wasn't sure if she could trust him around another girl on prom night. This made me so mad! We had been best friends for twelve years and he had only been dating her for three months. I felt like he didn't care about me anymore. I tried not to let it bother me and I got set to just go to prom with a group of friends. I know, I know: loser. Whatever. So the night before prom I got a phone call. It was Jason. He told me to look out my window...and there he was! No, he wasn't wearing a tux or carrying roses, but that didn't matter. I soon found out that he had been talking to my parents a lot to make sure that I didn't get a date to prom. That's not what it sounds like! He wanted to make sure I hadn't gotten a date; he wasn't trying to keep me from getting a date! And since I didn't have one, obviously, my parents helped him fly up and surprise me. Prom was the best night of my life (so far)! We have not been dating since then,

and he still has the same girlfriend, although I don't know why ;-).
But we talk more now and I realize that he cares a lot about me and he
is truly the best friend I could ever ask for.

Julie, in this next story, has this important message: "GO TO
PROM!! YOU DON'T WANT TO MISS IT!! ** Even if you don't
have a bf/gf...Grab a friend and go...It's worth it!**" And she's right.
I have been pushing the crushes-to-couples theme. I have mentioned
the link with graduation. But we must not forget that prom night is
also a big fat party, especially if it's your senior prom. Friendship is
deeply important to this party because it may be the last time you and
all your friends are together. Because of this, prom night is, among
other things, a celebration of friendship.

Julie, Sylvania OH (senior prom)

I know it has been more than a year now since senior prom, but it was
a night I will never forget :).... Well, my prom was on May 1st, but
preparation started a long time beforehand, back in September of my
senior year. I was a big fan of the movie *Titanic,* so I had decided to
make myself a gown from the movie. It took me the whole 8 months
to do it, but in the end it was finished and I was sooo happy! Well,
then I needed a date, and I was afraid to wait for someone to ask me,
so I took matters into my own hands and asked my friend Steve (who
was a junior at the time), to go with me. Well, I asked him four
months in advance, just in case. He said he would :).... He also
humored me, and bought a tux with the tails and all, so we could go as
"Jack and Rose." Meanwhile, about a month before the big day, I had
developed a relationship with another guy, Ryan. So now I had an
interesting problem. I wanted to go with Ryan, but I didn't want to
brush Steve off. My friend Crystal solved the problem for me though.
Since she was Ryan's best friend, and the one who introduced us (and
also in need of a date for prom), she asked Steve to prom. There,
problem solved :).... I asked Crystal if I would be able to dance with
Steve during prom, and she said of course!! Hehe...I was soo happy!

So now I was ready for the big night, none of my friends were hurt, and I was going with my boyfriend. I couldn't wait! We went as a group, me & Ryan, Steve & Crystal, and two of our other friends, Walter & Naomi. No limo for us cheapskates though, hehe.... We "vanned" it. Prom was absolutely awesome; it started at 6:30. It was held at the Wyndham Hotel. We had dinner first, then dancing 'til midnight. Being the goofy people we were, we had many amusing instances throughout the night, such as guys trying on our lipstick and shoes! And during a partner change (from me & Ryan to Crystal & Ryan) the guys decided to dance with each other for a song...Very interesting!! We had a blast!!! After the dance was over, we had an after-prom party at the high school. Games, food, and prizes! But by 3:30am, we were tired and ready to crash, which was meant to happen at my house. The night was over...but it was a night I would never forget! The moral of this story is, GO TO PROM!! YOU DON'T WANT TO MISS IT!! **Even if you don't have a bf/gf...Grab a friend and go...It's worth it!**

☆ ☆ ☆ ☆ ☆

Last but not least, a story that is truly and only about friends. Hooking up, the crushes-to-couples theme, even the need to go with one's bf or gf rather than a friend—these are absent from Eternity's narrative. Indeed, Eternity insists that going with friends is the best. And her prom night is in no way diminished.

Eternity, New Bern High, New Bern NC (junior prom)

At my junior prom, my best friend and I agreed to buy a couple's ticket to save money. We had each found really nice dresses and we knew we'd have a great time. One of my guy friends, CJ, offered to drive us to our dinner place and then to prom. At the restaurant we met up with a bunch of our closest friends. None of us had really serious commitments to anyone, and everyone was going to the prom as friends. We had a great time at dinner, laughing and talking. We even made several people smile at us and one elderly woman commented on what a great time we were having. We took a couple of pictures and then headed to the prom. The decorations were totally beautiful and all our other friends, who had other dinner reservations, were already at the prom. All of us—me, Liz, Sarah, her date, CJ, our other guy friends and their dates—danced with each other and in groups. It was really special to me because I am a socially inept person and parties are usually a nightmare. But that night I had the best friends in the world to share the night with. No one made fun of or tried to hurt anyone. We didn't need sex or alcohol or drugs to have a good time. All we really needed was each other. This year, I'm a senior, and I'm going with a good guy friend of mine, while Liz—my best friend—is going with my boyfriend because that's what we agreed to do in November. I know this year will be just as good. As long as I have my friends, prom will be a great experience.

Boyfriends and Girlfriends

Not everyone who goes to prom attends with a crush or goes with friends. Boyfriends and girlfriends also attend prom together. However, because they are already going out, and may have been for months or years, their relationships operate on a higher level than those of crushes and friends. What prom night does for them must, correspondingly, happen on a higher level. We can understand this "level" idea better if we see it as a function of tightness. Friends are OK tight. Crushes that transform into couples get tighter—they admit they like each other as more than friends. Boyfriend-girlfriend pairs must therefore get tighter still—they have already admitted they like each other, so now they must cross the threshold from like to love. There's no mystery in this. The transformational process from crush to couple is just as active in boyfriend-girlfriend pairs, except that it runs on a parallel but higher plane. You will see exactly what I mean when you read the story below: they are already going out; that they like each other is understood. Now, it's just a question of his admitting his love—and it's prom night that sets the stage for the admission.

Ashton, Lowell AR (his senior prom)

Prom is always one of those amazing nights when you come home and your head is swimming with how much fun you've had. But this prom was a prom to remember. I have been dating my boyfriend for about 3 months and it's been one of those relationships that develop very quickly. We've gotten very close, and I care about him very much. About a month ago one of my friends fell and broke his leg, and it really upset me. We went to the hospital together and then my boyfriend came and got me and I spent a long time crying on his shoulder. I don't know why I was that upset, but he understood, and as he held me my feelings deepened. Although I started to realize that I had fallen in love, I also believed that he probably didn't feel the same way. He's two years older than me, and well, after 2 months, it just didn't seem like he could feel the same way. I stayed awake at night thinking about this, and talked to my best friend about it. It bothered me almost constantly.

Finally prom night came, and my boyfriend picked me up and we spent an amazing evening together. We had such a good time dancing together and just hanging out. Afterwards, he took me to a park near my house and he said, "Ashton, I have to give you something." He told me to open the glove box. Inside was a card. On the front was a smiley face and it said, "Why is this card so happy?" Inside it said, "Because you're holding it. My turn next." He had written beautiful things inside it, too. Then he handed me a pastel pink rose...my favorite. I gave him a huge hug and he said, "One more thing...I stayed up until four in the morning writing this for you." He handed me a piece of paper. It was titled, "What I Feel for You." It was the most beautiful poem I've ever read. He talked about how the smallest things reminded me of him, and how our simplest hug made his heart melt. I looked up at him, and it was all I could do not to cry, and he touched my face, and said, "I love you." Then he kissed me, and if I didn't feel like Cinderella before, I certainly did then. It was a night to remember! =) Hope you all had as much fun as I did!

In this next story we again see how boyfriend-girlfriend pairs experience prom night at a higher level than do crushes. The transformational process is just as active, and feelings are what is being transformed—they either go from like to love, as they did in the story you just read, or, as in the story you are about to read, they go from love to a promise of unending love. Sometimes, there's even a ring involved, just to seal the promise.

Shakia, Escondido CA (senior prom)

The theme of my prom was "Forever Starts Tonight." I was going with my boyfriend, Gabe. It was also going to be our one-year anniversary.

I designed my prom dress and my mom made it. It was skin tight and very provocative, but my mom didn't mind. I chose a metallic pink material because no one was going to wear that color.

The day came and I was very excited. I was still getting ready when the doorbell rang. It was Gabe, early by fifteen minutes. My mom greeted him and took him into the living room. She wouldn't let me see him until I was completely ready. I felt like a bride. I was also a little embarrassed because I had never made my boyfriend wait before. When I finally came out and we saw each other, we were both speechless. He looked so handsome in his black and white tux. He looked more amazing than ever. He told me I looked beautiful. He couldn't take his eyes off me.

My mom took tons of pictures, then we left in the new Dodge Viper his parents had gotten him for his graduation. We drove to his friend's house so he and his girlfriend could follow us to the Hawaiian restaurant where we'd be having dinner. At the restaurant there were many people from our school, all of them dressed up. Everyone looked great!

Then we went to the dance and had a wonderful time. This was also the first time I actually danced with my boyfriend, and it turned out he was a wonderful dancer. The best-dressed couple contest was held and Gabe and I won. I was so happy because we really tried hard to stand out.

After the dance we went to this one party, but after a while Gabe insisted that we leave, so he took me to the beach and told me to walk to the end of this one wall. At the very end I found a beautiful bouquet of roses, with balloons, and a card that said, "Happy Anniversary." I was so surprised. Then he took out a ring and put it on my finger and said, "With this ring I promise you my love forever...starting tonight. I love you." I felt like the luckiest girl on earth. We sat on the beach for what seemed like hours, just holding each other and drinking in the night. At last we went home, and that night I had wonderful dreams. By the way, the ring was precious, and NO we did not sleep together, just in case you're wondering.

I wish I could repeat that moment of my life again; it was all perfect and very special.

Having a boyfriend or girlfriend also means that you have a certain amount of responsibility toward that person. Although not married, you are no longer single; you now have two of you to think about, especially when it comes to public, formal events like prom night. As her boyfriend says in the story below: "What's the point of having a boyfriend if he can't be there for you for the little things like your high school prom?"

Jillian, OKC OK (junior prom)

First of all, it was my junior prom, so I wasn't placing much importance on it. But, my boyfriend didn't go to his when he was a junior (he graduated two years ahead of me), so he really encouraged me to go, and promised me he would come, if he could.

The "if he could" is because my guy is in the army, and he had been hearing rumors that they would be leaving to go to the Middle East.

Time passed and prom crept up on us. The week of prom, on Monday, he got his orders. On Sunday of that same week, his brigade was leaving for Iraq. He told me he wouldn't be able to go to prom with me because the base puts the men on "lock-down" 48 hours before they leave. Perfect timing, huh?

I had everything ready...he had even gone dress and shoe shopping with me without complaint...the works.

A group of my single girlfriends were all going out to eat before prom, then were going out after prom, so I just planned to go with them. I'd already bought the perfect dress and the shoes, so why let them go to waste, right?

But on Friday evening, while doing my hair and make-up, my spirits were so down. If I hadn't spent as much on that dress I probably would have just decided not to go, and stayed home and finished off that carton of chocolate ice cream in the freezer. ;-)

My sister came over and helped me get ready, and after all the finishing touches were done, she reminded me to go put on perfume. I told her I already had, but she got flustered and said, "Well, go put some more on—you wanna smell amazing."

I was confused but said okay, and went back to my bedroom...

And when I came back into the front room, my boyfriend was sitting on the couch, wearing his "greens" (military dress), as well as a huge grin.

Needless to say, I had a few minutes there when I could barely speak because my smile was so huge. :D After I had settled myself down a bit I asked how he was off the base when he wasn't really supposed to be. He said that one of his commanding officers knew where he was, but "didn't know," if you know what I mean; and if my boyfriend had got caught off base he would have lost the new rank he'd just acquired the week before.

I didn't find out until the day after prom that my mother and sister had been in on it—they knew he was coming! At 3pm on Friday (the day of prom!) he decided he was taking me, no matter what, and so he had called my mom and told her.

To me, this is the kicker: my mom was worried about him getting in trouble and told him not to worry about me and my prom, and you know what he said? Just the simplest, sweetest thing, and even more so because he is my first "serious" boyfriend—he said, "What's the point of having a boyfriend if he can't be there for you for the little things like your high school prom?"

I'm a lucky girl. Needless to say, we had an amazing time and were rather the center of attention because he was the only guy there in a military uniform. :-)

Let's see, on prom night, new couples are formed, boyfriends and girlfriends get tighter than ever before, and yes, ex-boyfriends and girlfriends sometimes get back together as prom night makes them realize their true feelings for each other. This next story is all about getting back together. Poor "Nasty," though. You can't help but feel a little bad for her....

Lydia, THS, New York NY (his senior prom)

I was asked to prom last year as a sophomore. Tyler, the kid that asked me, wasn't altogether cool, but he'd just been dumped and well, so had I. He asked me because he knew I already had a dress and that since the break up, it would just sit there. Tyler and I went and had a great time until I saw my ex. Elijah (my ex) and I had been together for almost a year...and we did everything together, including a vacation to Hawaii. It was gut wrenching to see him with another date, especially since she was so nasty. Well, later on in the night, Tyler knew that I was bothered by seeing him and his "nasty" date together. Tyler was in a great mood because he had found his previous girlfriend and they had talked and were now "back together." I let them share a dance and decided to drown my sorrows in some punch.

I was standing talking to a senior girl when I felt a tap on my shoulder....I turned around to see Elijah, who simply looked into my eyes and said, "She's not as beautiful as you. You could make the stars fall, the sun rise, and any man alive happy." Then he kissed me on the cheek and left. I stood there for a good three minutes, completely confused. I began to cry because I was so miserable.

After Elijah said that to me, he went back over to the "nasty" girl and started hanging all over her. Tyler came over and led me back to the dance floor, where I did my best to have a good time while the "nasty" girl flashed me an evil eye most of the night. I decided to head to the bathroom because my punch was kicking in, and to my surprise there was "Nasty." She cornered me and started telling me about how bad I looked in my dress, and that she had plans to seduce Elijah tonight and that there wasn't a thing I could do about it.

I was devastated. I walked out of the bathroom...make-up running down my face from tears, and Tyler asked me what happened. Since he was like my best friend, I told him everything she said. He got so furious...he grabbed his girlfriend's arm and took her to the punch table with him..."Nasty" was there giggling her stupid giggle...then Tyler's girlfriend told her her dress was absolutely beautiful...and right after, Tyler took his RED punch, spun around, and dumped it right down the front of her LIGHT PINK dress! His girlfriend did her best "nasty" girl giggle...and said, "Oops, too bad for you. Lydia looks better anyway."

"Nasty" girl, in a fit of rage, ran across the ballroom, found

Elijah, and demanded for him to take her home so she could change. I was standing off to the side and could see everything. Elijah slowly walked over to me, grabbed my hand, walked back to her and said, "Find your own way home, I'm here with the right person now." Everyone laughed and clapped. To make the event even better, as "nasty" girl was leaving the building, she was running, and she tripped and fell and completely wiped out in front of all 2,000 students. Tyler and his girlfriend and Elijah and I all double date now. Elijah and I have been together now for almost three years (except for the week break-up for prom). We will be attending my senior prom in a few months.

More Crushes to Couples

With this next set of stories, we get back to romance and hooking up. At risk of sounding obvious, I want to point out, once again, that prom is a process. It takes place in the feelings; it channels these feelings, develops and forces them into the open. Throughout this book, I have called this channeling the "crushes-to-couples" process. This next story is all about this process. I chose it because it illustrates how two friends can like each other for years, yet never act on their feelings. Indeed, if it were not for senior prom, they might even graduate without acting. In this story, then, we see just how prom can work as the catalyst that brings these two people together. It is important for this process that prom is also about endings and transition, from junior to senior year or from high school to college or work. Prom night is a vivid reminder that time is about to run out, the school year, or high school, ending. Psychologically no doubt, this accounts for at least some of the pressure that drives the crushes-to-couples process—as time runs out old friends begin to feel that if they don't hook up now, they never will.

Laurie, Jackson MI (senior prom)
My guy friend (John) and I began planning prom four months in advance. We were best friends and had known each other since junior high. Throughout high school, and especially senior year, we would always joke about going to prom together, but we never seriously thought we would. He was very popular and good-looking, so he'd pretty much always had girlfriends. I wasn't ugly or anything, but for some reason, I'd had terrible luck with guys. John had now had the same girlfriend for two years. They seemed truly happy together. Me, I'd been single the last two years.

Eventually, prom was one week away, and I still didn't have a date. John and I had promised each other that we would take a limo to prom, him with his date, and me with mine. But since I was dateless, all the picture-perfect things we'd planned four months in advance seemed to be fading further and further away. I tried to tell myself that I didn't care, and that prom would still be fun even without a date, but my emotions were telling me differently and I wanted to go with a date so bad.

Deep down I wanted to go with John, whom I'd secretly been in love with since day one. But because of his girlfriend, that was obviously out of the question.

Prom was on Friday, and the day before, Thursday, I broke down in school. Everything was going the wrong way for me. Not only was I dateless. I also couldn't take seeing John with his girlfriend any longer. My feelings for him had been covered up for so long that honestly, I didn't even know how strong they were. I was so completely overwhelmed with unhappiness that day that I left school early. I had to calm down.

Just as I was leaving, John stopped me in the hall. He asked me where I was going, and if I had time later that afternoon to get together and talk. I told him I was going home and I assured him that I had time for him.

He came over late that afternoon and the first thing he said was that he and Jamie (his girlfriend) had broken up. I began asking a million questions. I was breathless and for some reason really agitated, thinking this was like, the worst thing that could have happened to him.

He saw my reaction and he tried to put what he was saying on hold. He didn't know what, but he knew there was something wrong with me and he wanted to make me feel better.

I said that I would tell him what was wrong after he finished telling me about Jamie. So he said that he had to break up with her because he just couldn't take the strain anymore. His next words were, "Laurie, ever since I've known you, I've thought you were amazing. Your personality, your beauty, everything. I've been torn about telling you this for a long time. Jamie was my girlfriend of two years and it was great, but the feeling I get when I see you is incomparable." He said it wasn't fair to Jamie and that he had to let her go.

He then asked me if I would accompany him to prom.

I began to cry. Tears seemed to flood the room. I must have cried for at least ten minutes. I just couldn't help myself, and I couldn't tell if I was crying with happiness or what. At last, when I was able to speak again, I said that this must be unreal, using exactly those words. John was taken aback at my reaction and wasn't sure if it was a good or bad one.

I couldn't help laughing when I saw the hurt look he gave me. I told him that I'd liked him since forever and that I'd tried to stop my feelings, but nothing worked. That's why, I said, I'd left for home early that day, because I just couldn't stand seeing him with Jamie anymore, especially with prom one day away and all our plans ruined.

We talked some more about how I'd felt all these years. He told me that he had felt the same, although it had grown more in the past year, and we laughed at all the time we had wasted. At one point he said that we had not wasted it after all, "Because all this time I was getting to know you better without any boyfriend-girlfriend pressures." I thought that was so sweet!

It was nearly midnight when he left. We never kissed that night, though, or officially started a relationship. Without saying anything, it was like we both agreed to wait until prom night.

You know, I never thought anything good could come into my life. But that Thursday night before prom I realized good had already come to me, and that it was John. I literally felt like God had smiled down on me. We went to prom and had an amazing time...everything we had planned together over the past four months worked out perfectly. All my dreams seemed to come true that evening and I had never been so happy. We ended a fabulous night with our first kiss and the beginning of a new relationship. We have been together ever since and plan on keeping it that way!

The next story is another version of the one you just read. She's asked a number of different guys to prom and they've all let her down in one way or another. She finally decides to go with her friend, whom she's known since eighth grade. Her understanding is that this is a fallback measure, even though she's been attracted to him (and he to her) pretty much since they met. Well, now it's prom night, the crushes-to-couples process kicks in, and you can imagine what happens next.

Amber, Virginia Beach VA (junior prom)

I had it all worked out. I was going to prom with a guy I had had a crush on since my freshman year...little did I know he had other plans. After telling me that he would go to prom with me, he decided that he wanted to take more than one girl. Then when I confronted him about it, I was dumped. OK, not really off to a good start, huh? So then the other guy I'd had a crush on since my freshman year said that he would take me to prom. Great! But then this guy, who is also a musician, decides that he is going to get a gig that night...it's about three days before prom.

The entire time I had been chasing after these guys, my best friend had been begging me to let him take me. Having known him since eighth grade, I never really paid much attention to the fact that there was an attraction going on between the two of us. Even though I sensed it, I was deathly afraid of it. He was my best friend and I didn't want to jeopardize that relationship.

Well, since all my other windows of opportunity had seemed to close, I decided that it wouldn't be so bad to take my best friend to my prom. Well...I have never had a better time in my life! Towards the end of a night full of laughter as he stepped on my feet constantly (he was trying to show me how to dance, and I still can't), he told me that he loved me. For the first time, he had expressed his feelings for me (which apparently he also had had since eighth grade). I knew I had had an attraction to him since our freshman year, but I had chosen to ignore it. We were both terrified of what was going to happen, especially since I wasn't allowed to date!!!!!!!

So we agreed not to get involved. That lasted about an hour.

By the time we were on our way home, he leaned over and kissed me for the first time. I will never forget the way that kiss felt! That was the first beautiful moment of our relationship. The second was when we asked my parents if we could be together (this is about a month later). They arranged to meet us at the beach the day after I asked them. As I stood there getting ready to go in the water with my "not-quite-yet-boyfriend," my dad pulled me over to the side and told me that he and my mother were so happy that I had finally chosen the right one (this was the approving statement!). I ran into the water to tell my "now-official-boyfriend" that we were all right.

You should have seen the look on his face—that was the second beautiful moment! We've been together ever since. Our relationship is the most beautiful thing of all!

The next story is one more version of the two you just read. Stacey and Stanley are friends, although she's a junior and he's in college. Originally, Stanley was her brother's friend and she's had a crush on him "forever." She's never told him, but he knows—which probably means he likes her too. And so it's up to her junior prom to bring the two of them together.

Stacey (junior prom)

My prom night was the best EVER!! I will never forget it. See, I was a junior. And the guy I liked was in college. He was my brother's friend. I had had a crush on him forever. And I had never told him but I kinda figured he knew. Everyone called him Stanley. He was on the football team in high school and he was tall and handsome and he had muscles. He was like my dream guy. We used to hang out a lot I guess. He would come over to visit my bro and we would end up talking for hours. We got along really well. He was the one and only guy I wanted to go to prom with. But silly me I was too scared to ask him. So one day...me and Stanley and a bunch of my friends were all hanging out and me and Stanley were playing around and flirting. The subject of junior prom came up, and all of my friends had dates. It was about a month before the prom. And so I told all my friends I still didn't have a date and they knew I liked Stanley. So they said, "Hey, Stanley, why don't you take Stacey to her prom...you guys could go just as friends." And he looked down at me (I was lying on his legs) and he said, "If she wants me to I will." And of course I said YES!!!

So we made all these plans for all of us to meet at the school and everything. And I got the PERFECT prom dress. And he got his tux. He even rented a limo for me. And the night of the prom I was so nervous I thought I was gonna throw up all over him. I kinda didn't wanna go anymore...just because I was going with him...but I had to—

he had done all of this for me. So I heard the doorbell ring and my brother went to get it. And I heard them all talking downstairs and it was just like in the movies...I walked down the stairs and my mom was taking pictures...Stanley looked great. Then off we went. We ate at a fancy place and we went to the prom. We danced all night long. I loved to dance slow songs because I seemed to fit in his arms perfectly (even though I'm only 5'2" and he's around 6'). And on the VERY last song of the night...we were dancing to the song "All or Nothing" by Otown...Stanley pulled away a little bit because I had my head on his chest...and he looked down at me with those adorable blue eyes...and he kissed me. It was like fireworks went off in my head. I don't think anyone will ever kiss me the way he did. That's why I will never forget my prom night. We went to the prom and have been dating ever since. Now we are planning my senior prom and I can't wait!

This next story is all about the decisive moment. He's still a little shy. It's yet undetermined whether they are officially boyfriend-girlfriend. It's also the last dance. She's had more experience than him. So she puts her finger gently on the side of his chin, turns his face toward her, and kisses him on the lips, instantly addicting him to kisses. Process complete. Going out now. Thank you, prom.

Diana, MA (senior prom)

I took my boyfriend to my senior prom, which fell on our one-month anniversary. We were taking our relationship VERY slowly because it was his first, and because my last relationship ended in a really nasty way (I found out the jerk had a steady girlfriend the whole time we were together).

Anyway, the very day I vowed to never go out with a high school kid again, I see a sophomore, my (future) boyfriend, up on stage trying to make the drama club laugh with a spontaneous comedy skit he was doing. Without even knowing it, I was on full-crush-alert, and actually offered to join him and his friends in doing the skit in front

of the WHOLE school the following week. Why? JUST BECAUSE I
NEEDED ANOTHER EXCUSE TO TALK TO HIM.

Did I admit to myself I had a crush on him? No. Hehe. The skit
was an absolute HIT, and all my friends immediately saw what was
going on between us. Then, I'm in one of my rants about how our
school's "no date, no prom ticket" policy sucks, and my friend says to
me, "Why don't you ask (let's just call him Dave) to the prom?" My
response? "No way! Heck, man, that'd defeat the entire purpose
of...okay."

So I ask him. Five minutes of silence later, he says, "Yes." I'm
absolutely convinced he'll call me and change his mind, but he does-
n't. Rumor's all over the drama club that we're going out, and we
actually did a few times, but both of us were too chicken to consider
them dates. Then someone actually asks us, point blank, if we're
going out. My witty response: "I don't know."

So we decide we might as well go out, because we obviously
liked each other and had technically been dating for two weeks
already. I, always the cynic, and he, completely clueless on what to do,
didn't expect it to last very long, but we REALLY did like each other.

Come prom night, one month later, we'd realized that we had a
lot more in common than we'd thought at first, and it was lots of fun
being together, but we still hadn't kissed. We were still quite awkward
with physical stuff, so we decided not to worry about it. The last dance
of the night, they played probably the only "good" song all night, the
Beatles' "Places I Remember." My "boyfriend" and I get on the floor
and start slow dancing. Then, at one point, I put my finger gently on
the side of his chin, turn his face towards me, and kiss him on the lips.
He's startled at first, but relaxes after a while and holds me tighter.

Afterwards, he smiles and we keep dancing long after the song is
over. Then he offers me his jacket and we get ready to go to the after
prom party. I wore his jacket like it was a badge of pride. Like, "I'm
his."

Ever since then, he's been addicted to kisses and I love to wear his
jackets. We've been together for 11 months and counting, and it couldn't
be better. Next month's his junior prom, and we're excited to go.

(And if anyone makes another "Mrs. Robinson" joke, I'll send a
frowny-face emoticon your way :-).

Blind dates for prom are not always the best. Yes, the obvious reason is that you don't know the person. But it's not just the not knowing that's the problem. The real reason is that in getting to know each other over time, people are actually establishing emotional ties to one another. In blind dating, emotional ties have not been established yet. But because it is "dating," and the idea of dating comes with certain expectations, you feel you should expect the same kinds of behavior you'd get from someone with whom you already have such ties—that is, from someone you know. And when you don't get this behavior, everything goes wrong. By now, you probably suspect that the following story is all down hill. Except it isn't. Because she finds an old friend—the best kind of emotional tie—and true prom night kicks in.

Josie, Louden NH (senior prom)

It was my senior prom and since I didn't have a date, my brother had fixed me up with one of his friends from college. I had never met the guy and I was really scared! My brother had said his friend was alright looking, not bad for a college kid. Well, when he arrived, he was drop-dead gorgeous!!!!!! All I could say at that moment was, my bro is dumb, this guy's hott!

So we went to dinner. And it was horrible.

My date may have looked hot, but he was the worst mannered guy I had ever seen. He wouldn't talk while we were eating, just wolfed his food down. There were juices dripping down his tux and he burped three times. Then he asked if I was done with my food, and when I pushed my plate away in disgust, he ate all of it.

We got to the prom. We hadn't even gotten through the door, and he saw this really hot junior who didn't seem to be with anybody. He said he would be right back and walked over to her. In a few minutes, they walked inside together and I was left on the doorstep. I was furious, but there was nothing I could do and I just walked in by myself.

Fortunately, I found my best guy friend inside, whom it turned out also didn't have a date (I say "also" because I was already considering myself dateless, except that I had just been dumped and he hadn't). So the rest of the night I danced with my best guy friend—I'd never realized he would be that much fun or look that great in a tux (hott!).

Finally they announced prom king and it was he, my best bud! I was so excited for him! But since he didn't have a date I was like, I wonder who will get picked queen? Well, right after his, they called my name, announcing to everyone on the dance floor, "Josie M____ is prom queen." I almost wet myself! I didn't even move for like ten minutes, so my friend, now king, came down and took me up on stage with him and gave me my crown. I was so happy!

At the end of the night, something even better happened. My friend and I left the dance together, and he took me home because my "date" was all over this other girl—not that I cared at this point. So we pulled up to my house around 12:30 and I asked him if he wanted to come inside, but he said no, that he really had to get going. So he walked me to my door and we kissed. It was our first kiss! And, well, now we are a couple! I can't help smiling as I write this!

From Asking to Dating

In this next story Katie and her prom date are good friends—her best guy friend, in fact. It turns out he's liked her for a long time, but she hasn't returned the feelings. At least, not until he asks her to prom. As she says, "I guess it was his asking that actually made me notice him as more than a friend for the first time." I have insisted that prom is a process that takes place in the feelings, and that the culmination of this process is the transformation of crushes into couples. At this point I want to make it absolutely clear that the process doesn't necessarily begin or end on prom night. It starts as early as the moment someone is asked to prom, and it may not end until the first kiss, during the after-prom, or even later, once actual prom night is over and done with. The process doesn't work at the same speed in every couple. And prom night is but one part of the overall process, which may span months, from asking to finally hooking up. All that prom guarantees is that the process will be there.

Katie, Beverly Hills CA (senior prom)

I had my senior prom a few months ago. Oh, it was the most wonderful night of my life and I will never forget it! I had been asked to go by my best guy friend. I had said yes. He had asked me a few months before prom, and then over those next months I had begun to like him as more than a friend. I guess it was his asking that actually made me notice him as more than a friend for the first time.

Anyways, getting back to my story, the night was wonderful. My hair was done up perfectly (it took like four hours to do). I had the nicest dress, ice purple with black ribbon that tied it up at the front, and it was just brilliant. My makeup was fantastic. Everything was perfect, perfect, perfect! Anyways, me and my date had decided to go in a limo, although that's what everyone does. So I was waiting outside for him because he had called me to say he was about two minutes away, when I saw this horse and carriage turn the corner and pull up in front of me. He then got out with a blue rose and helped me into the carriage. He said he wanted this to be a night I'd never forget and that a limo was too normal, that no one would be doing this. I was speechless. Not just the carriage. But he looked so incredible in his tux! It was the first time I had ever seen him dressed up this way, and I couldn't believe he was my date!

Well, when we got to the prom, everyone was outside waiting for me (he must have told them we were coming by carriage). We greeted all our friends, then everyone went inside where we had an awesome time dancing. All through the night, my date and I danced close and looked deep into each other's eyes. If I thought I'd liked him before then, now I was just swooning in his arms—and yet he made no move. Throughout the entire dance, even when the last song came and I had my head on his shoulder and he was holding me so that we were tight, I thought he would kiss me, but it didn't happen.

And then prom was over. Me and him and about six other couples had rented rooms in a hotel not far from the prom place. We were all going to spend the night there (not have sex) 'cause we couldn't be bothered going home. I was sharing a room with my best girlfriend, and I went in to get something, my date following. And on my bed, there was a little box with my name on it. He told me to open it. Inside, was the most beautiful ring, with a tiny diamond and all this gold in like scrolls and waves. As I stood there looking at it, thinking it couldn't be real, he asked me to be his girlfriend, telling me that he had developed all these feelings for me. Yes, I cried, it was so sweet. Then he turned on my favorite slow song, and we danced. At the end of the dance, we kissed for the first time. It was the most romantic night of my life and we are still together four months later and we love each other heaps!

In the previous story she starts to like him after he asks her to prom. For them, the hooking up process begins at the moment of asking. It ends when he presents her with a promise ring and they share their first kiss. The next story follows the same trajectory, except that Carlos has only known the girl for a month. When his story ends, the crushes-to-couples process is not yet complete, although prom night is some days behind them (and yes, they had a wonderful time). As he says throughout his story, "It's a definite possibility that my date and I will start going out." So when will the process be complete for Carlos and his date? Exactly. When they finally hook up.

Once again, the crushes-to-couples process doesn't work at the same speed in every couple. And prom night is but one part of the overall process, which may span months, from asking to at last hooking up. All that prom guarantees is that the process will be there.

Carlos, Falls Church VA (junior prom)

I had my junior prom last week, on June 10. It was a great time and I'll remember it for the rest of my life. The day started simple enough. I woke up a little early so I could go get my hair cut and pick up my date's corsage at my school. My date was someone I had met the month before, and since then we had become really good friends. I liked her the moment I met her, and still do. It's a possibility we may start going out, but you never know. Anyways, after I got my hair cut and got my corsage, I had a lot of hours to kill before I had to get ready. We had originally planned on going to dinner, but neither of us had much money, so we decided to save the little we had for prom pictures. I went to the mall for the afternoon and then I came home around 6 pm, took a shower, and put on my tuxedo. At about 7 pm I called my date and told her I was leaving to go and pick her up. After getting the corsage, and some extra stuff, I left in my mom's brand new Neon. I know, some guys may not like that car, and it's not terribly expensive or hot, but I liked it because it has a nice little sound system.

I arrived at my date's house at about 7:30. Her mother is a really sweet and nice lady, and I talked to her for a while, as I waited. When at last she came into the room, I couldn't believe my eyes. She just looked so beautiful, and I was really glad that I was taking her to my prom. I put on her wrist corsage, and put my boutonniere on myself. Both matched in color and flower (white rose), so that was cool. After her parents took video and pictures, we went back to my house so that my parents could see us. They also took video and pictures. Done with all of that, we finally got on our way to prom. It was about 8:30 and prom was in the next town, 30 minutes away. It started at 9 so we were right on time.

When we arrived not many people were there, but the hotel and ballroom was decorated really nicely. It was all so elegant. We met up with a friend and his date, and we talked for a while. After about half an hour a lot of people started to pour into the hotel. My best friends showed up and me and my date joined them, talked a while, and then we all got a table next to the dance floor. After some more talking, we all went up to the dance floor. I had never danced to a fast song in my life, but I said what the heck, I'm gonna try it anyways, and I made my date do it too. Well, surprisingly enough, we were pretty good. We literally danced the night away, taking only a few breaks for drinks and more conversation. The slow dances were magical with her, and halfway through the evening we started holding hands. Now I know you're supposed to do that with your date and some people may think nothing of it, but it meant a lot to me because I already liked her so much, and my feelings seemed to be growing by the moment.

When they announced the prom court, my best friend won prom prince and my other good friend was prom princess. It was really cool to see my friends receive that honor. We danced some more, and finally when it was over, we said our goodbyes to everyone, and me and my date left the hotel, hand in hand. I then took her home. She asked me to come in. I did, and she and I talked with her mother (who surprisingly was still awake at 2am) for a while, telling her about how wonderful the night had been. At last, I gave my date a kiss on the cheek, wished her good night, and went home. All in all, it was one of the greatest nights of my life. I've never had so much fun. I was really tired from the dancing, but I didn't care. As I said, it's a definite possibility that my date and I will start going out. I think we will, since we've now been hanging together every day since prom.

In Carlos's story, it looks like they're going to go out, but hook-up will happen some time after prom night—and it will happen. In the next story, the hook-up date is postponed indefinitely. Riley, telling the story, pinpoints the beginning of the crush-to-couple process to that moment in the graveyard when he asks her to be his date to senior prom. But the final moment, when they do come together—that will only happen "one day." Is that when the crush-to-couple process, which began with her being asked to prom in the graveyard, ends? Yes.

Riley (senior prom)

My prom night was the best!!! I went with the guy I'd had a crush on for six years, Jason. He was a senior and I was a sophomore. He was my brother's best friend and both of our families were good friends. Jason grew up with me and my brother. He went to our church. All of us had always been good friends. And he had known I had a crush on him for years now. Everyone knew. But that wasn't a big deal. One night after church he asked to talk to me alone. So I gladly walked outside with him. It was outside in the church GRAVEYARD of all places that he asked me to be his date to his senior prom. And I accepted. I went out and got the most gorgeous dress in the entire world...dark red...it's kinda hard to describe but it was gorgeous. Well he picked me up and of course my parents had to take pictures. And we went out to eat and then he took me back to his house for some pics with his family, who I love to death. And off we went to the prom. It was just in his Jeep. No limo or anything. But it was nice. We danced all night long. He is a wonderful dancer and kinda makes u dizzy when ur done. But it's so much fun. I especially liked to dance the slow songs. Well he drove me home (my mom didn't like the idea of me going to after prom b/c I was so young). And we stood out on my front porch for what seemed like forever. And he looked into my eyes and leaned in and kissed me. OMG IT WAS THE BEST KISS EVER!!! Me and Jason aren't going out b/c he went away to college...but we both love each other a lot. I'm sure one day we will be together...and only b/c of that night he asked me to prom in the church graveyard. LOL.

One for Our Tomorrows

In this next story, Jess, who's telling it, is deeply steeped in the magic of prom night. Various levels and kinds of magic: the joy of friendship, the most special joy of having a boyfriend, the sadness that comes with knowing that this is the end of high school—even excitement as she wonders what the future will bring.

Jess, Nanaimo BC (grad/prom)

Wow, OK, prom had finally rolled around the corner. I had gotten my dress; it was a really light purple dress that poofs out at the bottom with sleeveless top, with gloves, tiara and a shawl (very princess-like). Anyways, me and my friends had made appointments two and a half months before grad and prom to get our hair done, nails, and everything else. I had no trouble getting a prom date since I had a boyfriend of nine months, so we knew we were going to prom together practically at the beginning of the year, whether we were still dating then or not.

So prom day had finally come. Yes, prom! The day I had been waiting for since I was like seven, and it just seemed so much like a dream 'cause I remember, when I was little, always talking to my friends about how prom was going to be such a magical night and how I wanted to look like Cinderella, lol. It seemed very unreal for me now that the day had at last arrived!

We all woke up that morning (five of us had stayed at my place that night). We showered and stuff then went to our different appointments. Me and Kirstyn (one of the girls) both had tiaras, so we had to get special hairstyles that would hold them in. The salon did an incredible job and our hair looked awesome! Everyone had brought her gowns to my place the night before. So now we all met there again after our appointments and put the gowns on. It was still a little early, but we were enjoying what we all felt was our last moment together, just the girls, before the dates arrived and the night began.

Eventually, we were all set and as the time for our dates' arrival got nearer, we went outside to wait for the limo. It came, and all our dates got out. They looked incredible! My boyfriend was awesome in his tux. They gave us our corsages and we took some pics, then all piled into the limo and cruised for a while. We were having the perfect time, and we kept standing up in the limo, poking our heads out of the sky roofs and stuff—it was TUNZ of fun! At one point, we all jumped out at Safeway because we saw other prom girls from our schools and we wanted to say hi. There, EVERYONE stared at us! I kind of felt dumb, all dressed up and jumping around while people looked, but we were being complimented on how we looked so awesome, so after a while I felt OK again.

Once we were done cruising we went to prom. We entered through the "Gateway to a Magical Night," which was the theme of our prom and which had been written above the gateway itself—an iron gateway decorated in flowers, with clouds above it, leading into the dance hall. Shortly after we got there, I had to go up to the stage and say a speech about how my school career had been and how I was going to miss everyone because I was moving to Beverly Hills to start college. Then they all cheered for Kyle (my boyfriend) to lead me in the first dance. Smiling, he took my hand and led me down off the stage onto the dance floor. Everyone surrounded us as we danced to "Back at One" by Brian McKnight. I was so happy at that moment that I started crying, although I felt dumb for doing so (and I didn't want my makeup to run). But Kyle pulled me closer and hugged me for what seemed like the longest, sweetest time.

The whole night was just so magical! Prom is everything you think it will be and more when you're a little girl! To all my friends, it's so weird that prom is finally over, and that we made it this far together. It's so weird, and now we're all leaving home to go to college, going our separate ways in life. It was bound to happen. But it makes me sad. So just know that you guys were always the best to me, and the best friends a girl could ever have. And although it's sad to leave, I know we will make it far in life and meet again! AND to Kyle, hun: I truly love you and it hurts to leave you for the first four months. But in January when you move to California with me it's going to be the best, hun, and I can't wait. Until then, thanx for making my "Cinderella" night come true and being there for me as a wonderful boyfriend. I love you babe!

Short and Sweet

Let's close this section with two longs and six shorts. They are not necessarily central to our understanding of prom night. But like the frills along the edges of a rug, while they may not be central, they are undeniably a part of that rug.

Girls often go to more than one prom, and some may go to as many as three or four. The following story is about a girl's first prom. She is very young, but as she says, "I will always think of my first prom as the sweetest."

Lisa, MN (her first prom)

Last year I went to my first prom. I was very young to go, too. I was only a freshman and 15 years old. But I got asked by the guy I really liked then, who was a junior. I wish we would have gone out, but it never happened. However, we are still good friends now.

He asked me to be his date about seven weeks before prom night. He was so nervous asking me that it was really cute.

I got the perfect dress that I wanted. I got my hair done really nicely with little flowery clips in it. I got my makeup and my nails done, too. Everything was going perfect!

My date came to get me at two to take pictures at our houses and at the school. I was soooo nervous when he came to the door and I could tell he was too. He came in, and when he saw me he said I looked really great. Then he took my hand and put on my wrist corsage. Then we went to take pictures at the school and at his house.

At five we went out to eat, just the two of us. It was great but there were some silent moments since we are both kinda shy. But I was so nervous I hardly ate.

Then we got back for the Grand March in our school, where they announce each couple and you have to walk across the stage. That was embarrassing and scary but kinda fun. Finally, from nine to twelve we went to the dance in our gym. The gym had been decorated very beautifully and it took your breath away when you walked in. I danced with him to every slow song except one, when another guy, who I really like now, asked me to dance.

After that, we went to his house and watched movies and talked until about three thirty in the morning. Finally, I went home.

Now that I look back on it, that was a really awesome night! The only thing that could have been better was if my friends had been there, cuz only two of us in ninth grade went and we didn't know each other very well anyway. But his friends realized that I didn't know anyone else there, and so they were really nice.

Now, I just hope that I get to go to prom this year again, and that I have as wonderful a time! But I will always think of my first prom as the sweetest.

Heather, IL (junior prom)

I'd had a crush on this guy, Jake, for a long time. It started when I was a freshman and he was a junior. Although a freshman, I had a date to junior prom—no, not Jake. Jake promised me a dance, though. But he spent the whole night with his date, and I was with my date, so we never got around to it. Then after the dance when all the lights were turned on and everyone was clearing out of the ballroom, I walked up to him and said, "You owe me one big time, Mister!" He looked at me, and I looked at him, then he grabbed my hand and dragged me out into the center of the floor, underneath the chandelier, and held me close. We danced together for what seemed like an eternity while he sang in my ear. He finally ended it with a kiss on my cheek. A Kodak moment!

I know what you want to hear: "We all lived happily ever after, and I got the guy." Yeah, right! A year went by, and as romantic as the moment sounded, it didn't last. It was my sophomore year, and Jake's senior. We always remained friends, and the night before winter ball we talked and I promised him a dance. Well, I was so caught up in my date that night that I completely forgot about my promise to Jake. I saw him right before the last dance, but then my date pulled me aside and we danced together. Afterward, though, Jake was waiting for me. And yet again...we danced, in the light all alone, only this time I sang into *his* ear.

Now it's my junior year, and I can ask anyone I want to prom, rather than having to go with someone older than me. I still like Jake. I always have, deep down. I asked him to go and he said yes, and we promised each other that no matter how much time we spend together during the dance, we WILL have our dance, in the light, under the chandelier, and everyone can watch, and this time we'll BOTH sing.

Caryn (senior prom)

Okay so it was my senior prom and I had had a crush on this guy for four years. He knew how much I liked him, but he had a girlfriend that he had been with for about six months. Anyway, he was crowned prom king and the night was almost over when they announced the first dance with the king and queen. Well the queen ended up being his girlfriend, and right as the music was about to start playing, I felt a tap on my shoulder. My crush was standing right behind me and asked me to dance with him. He had asked his girlfriend if he could dance with me and said that she should dance with another person for the first dance of the king and queen. I was so incredibly happy! That made my senior prom unforgettable.

Jazmine, Sioux City IA (senior prom)

I was a freshman in high school and I had the cutest boyfriend. He was a senior, quarterback for our school football team, center for our school's basketball team, and he was very considerate. We'd been going out for three years by the day of prom. I had gotten my dress, had my hair done, and was ready to go. As I waited at my house for him to pick me up, I noticed his car drive by—or what I thought was his car. I was beginning to think that this was all a joke and that he wasn't going to show up. As I walked through my kitchen I saw a little puppy sitting on my porch. I opened the door and around the puppy's collar was a red rose. I picked him up to bring him inside and he was sitting on another red rose. Well, there was a trail of roses leading to my family's gazebo, and inside it were three-dozen red and white roses. When I came out of the gazebo, my date was standing inside the house with my family. I'm not sure, but I think I started to cry! The night was perfect.

Abigail, EHS, TX (junior prom)

My date wanted me to save him the last dance. When it came that time, we had to leave b/c our limo had arrived. So we walked outside and while our limo driver stood next to the car, we shared our last dance outside under the stars on the dock that looked over the lake. It was so romantic. After the dance, he kissed me on the forehead and for the first time, he said, "I love you!"

Brandi, MB (senior prom)

Well, I was all ready and I was waiting for my date and when he showed up it was like magic. He was acting a little funny the whole night and I finally asked what his problem was and he assured me that there was none and that I should continue with the night. He went over to talk to some buddies and I was in the middle of the dance floor where my friends were all standing and I asked them to go sit and talk but they insisted that we stay there. Not thinking about everyone's weird behavior, I stayed. After about two minutes I heard a voice over the microphone. I knew that voice well. I looked up and there was my boyfriend beet red in the face talking about how much he loved me. I believe he said something along the lines of him loving me with all his heart for the last three years and that even though we were off and on at times that his heart still belonged to me. My favorite song by Paul Brant came on. Then my boyfriend walked up to me and got on one knee and opened a white ring box and said, "I promise to love you forever and be with you whenever you need me." I started to cry and I said I loved him too and we danced and stared into each other's eyes all night long. That was the best moment of my life so far.

Sarah, PS 118, New York NY (junior prom)

I was desperate for a date to my junior prom and I had almost no possibilities. Finally, I decided to go with one of my friends who I actually had a major crush on and asked him (I go to an all girls high school). Up until prom night, we were just going as friends. Then, the night of prom, he came to my house to pick me up and when I opened the door, he had a dozen roses in one hand and a jewelry box in the other. He told me that he had been in love with me for years and could never get up the nerve to ask me out, but that since it was prom night, he would rather go with me as a couple than just friends. I told him I loved him too, and we've been together ever since!

Allison, Roanoke VA (senior prom)

Prom night was definitely a night to remember. Everything was planned weeks in advance. My dress was bought, my appointments made, transportation arranged. Everything was set. My date was a friend of mine from way back, whom I'd had a crush on for two years, and he looked absolutely fabulous. Everyone complimented us on how great we looked together. We went to dinner at this REALLY fancy restaurant in Washington DC. They served things like filet mignon and angel hair pasta! The prom theme was "Save the Best For Last." We arrived at the hotel and the music was bumpin'. The second we got there, my date and I hit that dance floor (the slow songs were especially fun!). Well, the night went by sooo quickly and the DJ announced the final song. It was Vanessa Williams's "Save the Best for Last." At the very end of the song, my date kissed me, and right then we both knew we were going out. It was a perfect end to a perfect evening. I couldn't have hoped for a better night. It was magical. I had dreamt of that moment for years…and it finally came true. Now I'm just sad that I won't be able to go to any more proms!! :(

AFTER-PROM

Introduction

The Many Reasons for After-Prom

The after-prom party and the after-prom weekend have become an integral part of the prom experience. Like the moment of asking, they may even be more important to prom-goers than the "traditional" prom dance. Why so important? One reason is that the dance itself is quite short (8 to 12 pm on average), too short for many of those who want to hook up romantically to get up the nerve and pop the question—they need the extra time. Another reason is that those who have just hooked up romantically would certainly rather continue the evening and be with their date—now their official boyfriend or girlfriend—than merely go home after the dance. Another reason is that friends want to hang out together, and this may be one of the last times they will all be together if they are graduating. Another reason is that the end of the school year has come at last and heavy partying—dry or otherwise—is a wonderful way to release the tensions that inevitably develop over the preceding school months. Another reason is that after-prom provides a strong psychological counterpoint to the dance itself; where one is intensely formal, the other lets it all hang out. And still another reason is that in staying out all night (or weekend) during after-prom, prom-goers break the parental hold that grips them the rest of the year.

So there are lots of reasons, and this list is not exhaustive; moreover, different prom-goers have their own reasons, and they are not always the same. Ultimately, these will depend on who you are and how old you are, whether or not it's a junior or a senior prom, and what your intentions or expectations are concerning your date.

This Section's Focus

In the previous section of this book, most of the stories end with the couple hooking up as the narrative talks you through their evening and into after-prom. I won't repeat those stories here; you have seen by now what happens as the night develops and the couple draws closer, and I leave it up to you to imagine the feelings they experience as the evening unfolds. Instead, I focus this after-prom section on the variety and ubiquity of after-prom activities in North America. This section breaks down in four ways: Canadian after-proms and US after-proms; and school sponsored after-proms and informal after-proms. Each of these, while sharing in the overall essence of prom, has its own style and flavor, as you will see. However, before we get to this breakdown, I do wish to include a small chapter on sex.

Losing Your Virginity
and After-Prom

There's this belief that a huge number of prom-goers lose their virginity on prom night, or that if they don't lose their virginity, then they at least try like heck to. The belief is that prom *promotes* the loss of virginity. Is this belief accurate? Does it reflect reality?

Yes and no.

Yes, because roughly 27% of both guys and girls intend to lose it on prom night. No, because intention and actuality are two different things, and the number who actually will lose it is going to be less than 27% and more than 6%.

How did I get the 27% and the 6%? To get the 27% I ran two surveys on www.*The*PromSite.Com, one for guys and one for girls, each with the same question and answers:

Plan to lose your virginity on prom night?
If YES, with whom?
    * Boyfriend
    * Crush
    * Friend
    * Don't plan to lose it
    * Already lost it

Of 400 male respondents, 29% answered that they planned to lose it with either a girlfriend (15%), crush (9%), or friend (5%). Of 400 female respondents, 25% answered that they planned to lose it with either a boyfriend (13%), crush (10%), or friend (2%).

On the other hand, 36% of the guys said they did not plan to lose it, and 38% of the girls said they did not plan to lose it. In other words, fewer guys and girls plan to lose it than plan to keep it. So the belief that you have to lose it on prom night may be there, but it is a belief held by a little less than half of all male and female prom-going virgins.

As for those who already lost it (36% of the guys, 37% of the girls), they don't count because it obviously isn't "first time" special on prom night.

Next, to get the 6% I assumed that there's a difference between those who intend to lose it and those who actually do lose it. How big a difference? That is hard to say. The survey I conducted—Did you lose your virginity on prom night? Yes or no—said that 6% of prom-goers lost it on prom night. But the survey is suspect because the population that visits www.*The*PromSite.com is mostly people who are going to prom, not those who have been and have subsequently graduated.

So what's the bottom line? Percentage-wise, the number of prom-goers who lose their virginity on prom night is quite low. Statistically, it may be as high as 27% (doubtful) or as low as 6%, but is probably somewhere in between.

Now, what about non-statistical responses to the belief that prom night is for losing one's virginity? Over the past five years I have posted plenty of statements in the Sex Talk area of www.*The*PromSite.Com, and this has given me lots of non-statistical written responses. One of the statements was, "You're supposed to have sex on prom night." Here's a response that sums up the general attitude:

> You are never "supposed" to have sex. If you want to, fine. If you don't, that's fine, too. If any guy tells you differently, dump him.
> (Jessi, Friendship MD)

And another:

> Absolutely not!!!! Prom means that you're supposed to have fun, not that you are supposed to do something that you might regret for the rest of your life. And if the person you are going with makes you feel like you are obligated to do something sexually with him that you are not willing to do, leave with a friend, and dump that jerk. He doesn't deserve you. Don't give in to some scummy guy, do what you feel is right. Get someone that respects you!!
> (Anon, Somewhere)

If these non-statistical responses are representative of general thinking about prom night, it means prom-goers go to prom to have a fun
time, not to have sex or lose their virginity. For a few, sex may be part
of the "fun time" package. But for most, sex is not the best idea
because it will probably interfere with the fun time, and will probably
have negative consequences down the road. Mostly, though, it will
probably interfere with your sense of self-worth if you give in to
something that you think you "ought" to do just because you heard it
was supposed to happen on prom night. And of course, the saddest
thing about giving in this way is that you'd be doing it all for nothing,
because as it turns out, the majority of prom-going virgins do not
lose their virginity on prom night, and do not want to lose it on prom
night.

But prom-goers, adults, and everyone else sure talk about it a lot.
Which means? Which means nothing. It seems we have here a perfect
example of the often sharp divergence between what we say and what
we do—and we all know that words and actions don't always match up.

Finally, you have probably noticed that the quotes I supplied
above came from girls, and that, in fact, the concern over losing one's
virginity on prom night—or any other night, for that matter—always
seems to center around girls, or emanate from the girls themselves. Is
it true, then, that guys are unconcerned, or that they are the ones who
insist on it prom night (or any other night), and that this therefore
makes them the perpetuators of the belief that prom night is all about
sex? You know by now the answer is going to be no!

Some guys are rougher and more vocal about their sexuality than
others, but in the main they are as concerned about it as the girls. It's
like the statistics said, 36% do not plan to lose their virginity on prom
night, which is comparable to the 38% of the girls who also do not
intend to lose it. In fact, if I import the statistics from another survey,
we can see just how strong is the similarity in thinking between guys
and girls. In this survey I asked both sexes, "When do you plan to have
sexual intercourse?" There were three possible answers:

1) I will wait 'til marriage.
2) I will not wait 'til marriage but haven't had it yet.
3) I've already had it.

29% of the guys said they would wait 'til marriage, 31% said they would not wait, and 40% said they'd already had it.

33% of the girls said they would wait 'til marriage, 30% said they would not wait, and 37% said they'd already had it.

Guy or girl, the numbers are very close, which tells us that both have the same plans for their virginity, whether it's prom night or any other night.

So let me end this chapter with one guy's perspective on sex, prom night, and a few other important topics. What he's written is part of the ongoing dialogue in the Sex Talk section of www.ThePromSite.Com. As you read, keep in mind that his intended audience is teens just like him:

> First of all, I think this is obviously a touchy subject by the looks of other comments posted in this area. I can see both perspectives in this situation and think that if I explain my own situation to everyone, it might help a few other people reflect.
>
> My girlfriend and I have been dating for a little over 3 months now and believe it or not, we've been through a hell of a lot. I've always been the type of person who believes that sex is an action that should only be taken with someone whom you love with all your heart and that the only time you'd actually decide to make love to that person is when you're sure the time is right and that you'll be expressing your love for them through sex. That's just my opinion and I respect that other people have other opinions. As a matter of a fact, my own girl-friend has very different views on sex. She believes that it isn't anything serious and is just a form of pleasure that should be available whenever you feel like it.
>
> I guess it's because I have different views that it's kind of made her a bit cautious of me when it comes to this matter, because she's never met a guy who I guess you could say has a "typical girl's" perspective when it comes to sex. Because of our different views we've decided to wait; so, yes, we haven't made love yet. And without going into much detail, I'd appreciate it if no one were to comment as to my comprehension of the word love and whether or not I actually mean it when I say I am totally in love with my girlfriend. We have been through a lot,

good and bad. How bad was the bad? Enough to tear my heart into millions of pieces at the time and it still hurts when I think about it. But I'm still here for her, I still love her, and it's for that reason (and only that reason) that we're still together.

Prom is coming up next Friday and my girlfriend and I have discussed the issue a great deal. In fact, one of the things about me that makes me who I am is that I'm extremely over-analytical. I've analyzed this topic daily for about two months with her. I know that she's unsure of her emotions and how she really feels, and I respect that. If she were to say no, I would totally respect that and back off immediately—in fact, I have. But we decided that after prom we are going to get a hotel room. We've kind of mutually agreed that we're going to stop analyzing everything and just do what feels right. If by chance it doesn't feel right at the time, we'll probably just end up sleeping together in the same bed holding each other. I don't really care. I just love being with her and being close to her and that matters more to me than any other action. I want to be with her and although I do want to express how I feel for her through sex, that's something we'll have to decide together when the time comes.

I think everyone here who is questioning whether or not they should have sex should really think about it in a different way. I realize you're here to see other people's opinions and see if any apply to you, but I think the best advice anyone can give you is that you need to be at a comfort level with your partner where you can fully talk about it without being nervous. Sex is a very big issue to begin with; if you can't talk to your partner about it and discuss your concerns, then I don't think there's any question that you should even be having it.

Second, if you are at that comfort level with your partner where you can discuss all of your concerns and such, then I think you'll obviously have a better idea of what the real issue is. Prom is not all about reputation; it doesn't follow a "1. Dinner, 2. Dance, 3. Hotel to have sex" routine. Don't feel pressured into making unwise decisions simply because all of your friends might be. Talk to your date about it. Furthermore, I guess I'm giving this advice more to people that are like me. If

you're the kind of person who treats sex as nothing more than a simple action to feel pleasure, then there's nothing to say because your only issue is safety. But for anyone else, I just feel that people should look at all of the factors involved and talk them through before coming to a conclusion.
(Scott, Ottawa ON)

Sponsored After-Prom

It wasn't always this way, but today not only is there an after-prom, but the after-prom goes all night, and often into the weekend. In the past twenty years or so schools all over North America have recognized that prom-goers continue the party into the following morning, and many of the schools have tried to formalize the after-prom into a safe party for their students. "Safe" in this case hasn't always meant "dry." In Canada, schools sometimes sponsor after-prom parties that permit drinking—despite violating the legal drinking age of 18 or 19 (depending on the province). But they do so only under supervised conditions. In these instances, parties are usually held out in fields and on campgrounds, and school buses collect all the students and bring them (and their alcohol) out to the designated site. The thinking behind this is, if they're going to do it, they might as well do it under conditions in which they can't hurt themselves. All of which makes perfectly good sense.

In the US, sponsored after-prom parties are invariably dry. Prom-goers are anywhere between 15 and 18, and the US drinking age is 21. So sponsored after-proms don't have the choice. They are typically hosted at the school or in a rented hall, and parents and teachers chaperone. Sometimes the after-prom party has a theme and the place is decorated accordingly, or themed games are selected (the most popular being Casino Night); and sometimes it's just a collection of games and food—enough to keep the party going all night, and the prom-goers from getting into mischief.

Canada

The next few sponsored after-proms are Canadian. An after-prom party in a field, with bands and crowds and alcohol, is not unusual. Either the school arranges it or graduating students organize it themselves (with the school's blessing). Bear in mind as you read about the

Canadian after-proms below that prom has a slightly different meaning in Canada than in the US. In the US prom can be, but does not
have to be, linked with graduation. Its emphasis for prom-goers,
especially junior prom, is more on relationships and hooking up. In
Canada, on the other hand, prom is almost always linked with graduation. This brings with it a corresponding change in the psychology of
prom-goers and sponsoring schools alike: because it is about graduating and becoming young adults, why shouldn't "adult" activities be
permitted (or at least tolerated), and why shouldn't the grads be treat-
ed accordingly? Additionally, since the legal drinking age is 18 or 19,
depending on the province, and graduating seniors are themselves
between 16 and 18, the disparity between legality and actuality is not
large enough to worry about. Hence, the greater tolerance for drinking during a sponsored after-prom party.

Terra , Lasalle Secondary , Sudbury ON

After prom every graduate goes out to this huge field...over 500 ppl
go...it's a 3 day party and everyone camps out there. There are bon-
fires...live bands...and dj's set up all over the field...there's crazy
games to play like mud wrestling...and much more...THIS IS HOW
CANADA LIKES TO PARTY!!

Chic, Victoria BC

Our grad class is piling into buses that are going to drive us to a surprise place (so the party doesn't get broken). There will be music
there and it goes all night (last year it was on the beach). Best of all,
we all bring alcohol and nobody minds! SO FUN!

Jen, AB

We don't have a prom here but a graduation. It all starts off with the
cap and gown ceremony at 9am, then after a couple of boring hours,
you leave and get ready for grand march, which is where you and your
date's names are called and you get to show yourself off in front of
your friends and families. Only the grade 12s get to go to this since we
are the ones graduating. We have no dance or anything after this, but

instead we have a Safe Grad, where buses take us out to some farm-
land far away from the city, and everyone gets just drunk, until they
take you home at 7 the next day. It's a good time.

Casey, Foothill Composite High, Okotoks AB

We have what we call colour day on the last Thursday of June and that
is where the whole cap and gown and diploma ceremony comes into
play. Then the following day everyone gets dressed up in amazing
dresses and tuxes and we ride in a limo to Calgary, the city closest to
us. Usually we stop and take pictures at pretty places and of course we
stop at the liquor stores because legal drinking age is 18 in Alberta.
Then it is off to the dinner with our parents and a few speeches and
awards are handed out after supper. A little dance follows and then a
huge party that consists of probably 1500 people or more. This is an
all night drinking fest for everyone to enjoy at someone's property
and even parents and teachers come. Cars and tents are the beds for
the evening if you even sleep at all!!!!!!

Marie, Halifax NF

Here "prom" is grad. It's on a Friday night, but people usually get
together with their friends the night before and have a bbq and drink.
All the grade 12s and the grade 10s and 11s that have been asked as
dates don't go to school on Friday. The girls spend the morning getting their hair done, and make up and nails, then go home to get
their dresses on. Some people have their dates over to their houses
first to have pictures taken with the family and stuff. Then starting at
around 3 we have a "wine and cheese," where we go to someone in our
grade's house for drinks and pictures. Most years, everyone rents
limos or some kinda cool car, but this year none of my friends could
get limos, they were all rented, so we are renting a metrobus for the
day and decorating it with banners and streamers and window paint.
That brings us to one of the fancier hotels in the city. Then we have
"meet and greet" where everyone gathers in the lobby of the hotel for
pictures and stuff. The dinner starts at about 6:30, and after that
there's a dance. People usually stay for about two songs, the
father/daughter and mother/son dance, and the date's dance. Then all

the grads and dates leave for the after-grad party. We rent school buses to take us to wherever the party is, usually at some hall or something, and party and drink all night. Then the buses come back and pick us up at 8 the next morning. Some people leave throughout the night tho, and rent hotel rooms.

Kim, St. Matt's, Ottawa ON

After prom our school (the students) has organized an after-grad party. We rented a ski lodge at a nearby ski hill and we rented a dj, bouncers, and bartenders. You only have to be 18 to drink (God love Quebec!!) so we are going to party until about 3am when we have a bus scheduled to pick us all up and bring us back downtown, where my boyfriend and I have rented a hotel suite (with our own balcony...yay!) and we're going to stay up all night!! I'm SO excited!!!!! Only 5 days until PROM!!!!! :-)

Just so you don't get the idea that all after-proms are hard into the alcohol in Canada, here are a few that nicely balance the above.

Diz, Campbellton NB

The day after the prom is our Safe Grad night. There we stay up all night having fun! We rent the pool center and the movie center so it's only grads! At 6am, we all go to McDonald's to have breakfast! Then we sleep all day and party all night! Next morning, Grad day...we're officially Grads!

Elle, Halifax NS

Prom lasts until 12, then everyone rushes home and changes into something comfortable. Then we go back to the school and get buses to Safe Grad. This is a big party after prom everyone goes to in a hotel. The school puts it on so no one gets hurt by drinking and driving. There are a lot of fun things to do like swimming, sports, and eating. Safe Grad is usually over at about 6am so then everyone goes home!

Amy, DSS, Delta BC

Grad's on a Friday. We get the day off and everyone gets ready. Then the guys pick us up in limos and we all go to the school so all the younger people and parents can take pictures of us. Then we go downtown for dinner and a dance. Then we come back to the community center and we have Dry Grad. It's an alcohol free event. It's awesome. We have themes. There's a hypnotist, games and food. It lasts all night, then we all eat breakfast in the morning. Then we hop the fence and jump in the community center outdoor pool in our clothes.

United States

The next set of sponsored after-proms take place in the US, and their style tends to be a little different from the first Canada set. As I noted in the introduction to this chapter, because the legal drinking age (actually, the age at which you can purchase alcohol or sell it) is 21 and prom-goers may be anywhere between 15 and 18, US sponsored after-proms are always dry. Does this mean that Americans don't know how to party? By no means! As you will see in the sponsored after-proms below, a "safe prom" or "dry prom" can definitely be "off the hook."

Jess, Genoa High School, OH

Last year I was fortunate enough to go to prom as a sophomore. I had to spend all after-prom alone because once we got there my date ditched me to go with his friends! Some enchanting evening...anyways, we had an hour after the actual prom to get into some more comfy clothes, then get back to the school. In the hallways everything was TOTALLY redecorated; it didn't look like our school at all—paper and artwork on the walls, streamers, fake trees, Christmas lights, and every kind of food you could think of. The chaperones made cookies, and then we had Subway, Taco Bell, McDonald's, and other places too. There was a laser tag tent set up, and there was a big blow-up boxing ring with oversized gloves. It was a lot of fun. Karaoke, poker, card tables, stupid yet fun carnival games set up in the cafeteria, just

everything you can think of! Can't wait to go with my friends this year
and actually have fun doing the stuff!!!

Angel, Air Academy High, USAFA CO

Our after-prom is REALLY big. The parents of almost every
senior/junior contributes at least $50 and then sets up huge inflatable
courses (you know, Velcro wall, giant slide, obstacle course, etc.).
There are tons of prizes (last year I won a printer!), and about 50 lbs
of pizza is available. There are also booths to play carnival-type games
and a "gambling" area. The entire thing is a huge blast—it's almost
better than prom!

Danielle, Wauseon High, Wauseon OH

After prom our seniors' parents rent out the fairgrounds and we have
fun activities, blow-up machines, and lots of fun stuff like a haunted
house and rides. Then we have an old drive-in that no one uses so we
re-open that up for the night and watch that at like 4am. Then off to
the bowling alley where we can do bowling, singing, and some dancing. Then off to the high school for a breakfast at 9am…and then
home to sleep for the day.

Sarah, Baltimore MD

Well our after-prom is taking place at the Hard Rock Cafe. We are
having Casino Night and I bet it's going to rock. After that we go back
to our school and have breakfast and have door prizes. I can't wait for
prom to come.

Keira, Mira Mesa High School, San Diego CA

My school's after-prom is taking place at Boomer's Fun Center. It has
everything from video games to miniature golf to bumper boats to a
racecar track. I think it lasts until about dawn or so.

Alicia, Lake High School, Buena Vista SD

After the dance is done all the kids have until one o'clock to check in at the "After Prom." When u check in, u can't leave 'til five. We then just play games all night. We have laser tag, bumper cars, a moon walk, sumo wrestling, human Velcro, human bowling, inflatable obstacle courses, raffles, and much more. It's a blast!

Jess, Taconic, Pittsfield MA

Prom ends at II. Then we have an hour to get to a fancy place called Eastover, where the juniors and seniors stay 'til 6am and go swimming, horseback riding under the stars, win money, Jello wrestling, and all kinds of crazy fun stuff. Then the next day we don't have to go to school, so me and my prom group are going to Rhode Island to relax on the beach.

Informal After-Prom

I call it an informal after-prom because it is an event that is not formally sponsored by the school or the local PTA or other concerned group. This doesn't mean that the school or adult group is not sponsoring an after-prom party—they may well be. It's just that not everyone elects to go to the sponsored after-prom and many groups of friends would rather party on their own, especially if they are unsupervised.

School-sponsored parties resemble each other because you cannot vary the entertainment all that much within the confines of a hall or gym. The sponsors may theme the after-prom, or it may consist of activities like laser tag, human bowling, a hypnotist, or karaoke. Informal after-proms, on the other hand, are open to a much wider range of activities. Some of these depend on where you live—some L.A. prom-goers go to Hollywood or teen bars, those near New York go into Manhattan, and so on. Most after-proms, however, simply depend on what a group of friends wants to do. So yes, you can go run around all night long in a 24 hour Wal-Mart, or you can go midnight bowling in your gowns and tuxedos, or you can drive out to a pier to watch the sun rise (romantic), or to a beach, or gather at a friend's house for movies, and so on.

As you will see, this next set of "informal" after-proms shows just how wide the range of activities can be.

Shellie, Anderson-Shiro, Anderson TX

After prom a group of friends and I went to a 24 hour Wal-Mart and ran around like little kids. It was so much fun! We were trying to get kicked out, but everyone there just laughed and let us be. After we left Wal-Mart we went to an IHOP at like three in the morning and ate. It was the best night ever!

Samantha, New Orleans LA

After prom we all head down to New Orleans and spend the entire night on Bourbon Street. It has got to be the biggest and best after-prom party there is!!!

Ale, Kamehameha Schools, Haleiwa HI

Our prom is in Waikiki and I love to surf. There is a swell coming to the south side (where Waikiki is), so my friends and I are going out night surfing! It is really, really fun and the lights of Waikiki light up the ocean. It is really awesome.

Didi, Hartford High, Hartford CT

After prom, me and a whole bunch of my friends are going to one of the casinos out here in CT to have dinner and to play in this arcade kind of thing they have in it. No one is going to a casino so we want to be a little bit different....

Britt, NC

This prom, being my first, my friends and I (a group of sixteen people) will only be staying at prom for a short while. We're going to be going across the street to Center City Fest Live (Foofighters, Everclear, Wallflowers, Widespread, etc.) and meet the rest of the world there. The music fest ends at 12 and we have the limo till 1:30 am, so we'll end up driving around for a while or go midnight bowling (yes, in our prom dresses!). Then we're going back to our friends' where everybody will be spending the night, swimmin' and playin' pool! Can't wait!

Alisha, Menifee County HS, Lockett Frenchburg KY

We are going all-night four-wheeling with a bunch of his friends back in the woods.

Vivian, Boston Arts Academy, Boston MA

After prom we probably will go grab a bite to eat and then off to an after party or anywhere else but home! It's prom night! We gotta live it up! Our proms are always on a Saturday night, so maybe if there's a club open we'll go club hoppin'. All I know is I'm out to look 4 some fun!!

Blythe, Reed-Custer, Braidwood IL

After prom our group of fifteen is going to downtown Chicago dressed in our prom attire to eat and hang out, and the next day we are going to Six Flags!

Jamie, Lake Highlands High School, Dallas TX

OK, well after prom me and my group of about 12 couples, we went to my house to change clothes, because we didn't want to be all in our nice dresses and all. Then we all loaded up in about four cars and drove to Oklahoma about 2 hours away (trust me it was worth it), and when we got there we had a houseboat waiting for us. We were there to party ALLLL night long. It was great!!

Maravilla, North Atlanta High School, Atlanta GA

After prom, some of my friends are going dancing at a club, some are going bowling, and the rest of us are going to chill at a cafe in down-town Atlanta. It's going to be awesome!

Dave, Cedarville High School, Cedarville MI

Well, I live in a very small town. There's not really much of anything to do. So picking a perfect after-prom idea was hard. But I chose to take my girlfriend up to the top of a hill which is like a mountain, and no one knows about it. Go up there, and lay on a blanket under the stars. And we can talk. Then, go back to my house to watch a movie or two. And take her home at 5 or 6am.

Priscilla, Weslaco High School, Weslaco TX
Well, after prom a bunch of us are going to the beach. We're going to
rent a condo and spend the night. It's going to be a lot of fun.

Tara, Brick Memorial HS, Brick NJ
Our group of 14 is going to Long Beach Island because my date's parents have a house there. We are gonna be up all night partying away!
WHOO HOO!!!! Then we are going to spend the next day on the
beach enjoying the hopefully nice weather!

Beth, TX
Instead of a limo, we are renting an RV and taking that to prom.
After, we are driving out to the lake with our jet skis and camping out!

Holly, MI
We're going to my friend's cottage (all 17 of us) and camping out on
the beach. Who knows what's going to happen between midnight and
sunrise, but it'll rock no matter what!

Alessia, Spring Valley High School, Pearl River NY
After prom we are going on a teen prom cruise that has a combina-
tion of what all 16 of our limo group people wanted including: dance
club, comedy club, lounge, and a casino. That cruise comes back
around 4:30ish (am). After that the group splits up...about half of
the group is going to brave the prom/Memorial weekend traffic down
to the shore, while the other half (including myself), will be going on
an all-expense paid party bus to Six Flags (compliments of my friend's
dad). So while one group is driving, the other group is sleeping and
waiting for the following day when we are all rested to go to Six
Flags...this makes sense...wouldn't you say?

Rachael, MBHS, New York NY
Instead of following the traditional "after party crowd," my boyfriend
and I are going to a late night jazz cafe where we will enjoy live music

and great food. Then later in the morning, we're following the crowd after all...to SIX FLAGS!!! :)

Lisa, The Hill School, Pottstown PA
After prom my friends and I (and my boyfriend) are piling into a limo, and going bowling in our finery. Then we're going to a diner for some food, then back to my house to hang out and sleep! I can't wait!

Terrell, Carson High School, Los Angeles CA
After prom my date, my friends, and I are going to head off to a party at my friend's mansion in Hollywood. And after we're going to an all-ages club (yes in our prom clothes!). After that we're heading to the Santa Monica beach to watch the sun rise. We're going to have lots of fun, and it will be off the hook! Not only that, we're going to have bottles of Bacardi to keep the party going. 'Cause ain't no party like a C House party 'cause the C House party don't stop!

Valerie, American Heritage, Fort Lauderdale FL
I went with my boyfriend to a hotel and stayed the night in a $900 suite in Coconut Grove, MIAMI! It was incredible.

Pat, Edinburg High School, Edinburg TX
Well, it is going to be my last prom, so what my boyfriend and I have planned is that we are going to stay at the prom until 12, then we are going to a nice restaurant that we have reservations at. After we eat we are going to meet up with some friends and we are all going to rent rooms at the beach. We are going to go over good times, and have a lot of laughs. When we see the sun starting to rise, we are going to go outside and watch until full daylight. Then we are going to share a passionate kiss together and come home.

The House Party

If there is a traditional informal after-prom, it definitely has to be the house party. This is what you see in movies like *American Pie,* and the movies aren't lying to you. The house party is still the preferred after-prom activity prom night.

Now, this isn't the place to cite alcohol abuse statistics among teens in the US and Canada. Yes, there is a substantial amount of drinking during after-prom and into the after-prom weekend. I won't deny it. But the amount is perhaps not as high as we might believe. The typical after-prom house party may be a kegger, yes. But that doesn't mean everyone drinks. Among those who will, most won't get toasted. The only ones who do get toasted—barring a few accidentals— are those same teens who get toasted on other nights, too. And this is a fairly small number. You cannot blame it on prom night.

Brandi, King William High School, Aylett VA
HOUSE PAAAARRRRRTTTTAAAAYYYY!!!!!!!!!

Joshua, Deering High School, Portland ME
About 20 or so friends of mine and I are taking water taxis out to one of my friend's camps on an island and partying until the break of day. Or we are going to go to the huge all-senior party at a rented house that is amazing and partying there until it's broken up by the cops or we just can't party anymore!! Either way it is going to be the best night ever.

Niniqua, Villy, ON
Goin' to the after-party...there are three local schools with their proms that same night so all the schools are attending one house party. The guy who is having it goes to my school. His property is

huge and he has a pool, etc., so there is gonna be like 400 ppl there and it's gonna be a night to remember!!!

Nicole, St. Joseph High, Brampton ON

The tradition at our school is an after-prom party. Someone out in the middle of nowhere has it. They charge for tickets in advance for damage costs, etc. Everyone sets up tents so no one drives home a l'il tipsy. Our prom is in June so the weather's great for an outdoor party and a bonfire!

After-Prom Weekend

You saw how many prom-goers continue the after-prom into the weekend—they go to a Six Flags amusement park the next day, or to the seaside, or rent a condo, or go to a friend's parents' cottage, or camping. At this point, prom and prom night are simply diluting into one long party—not that there's anything wrong with that. I end this section with a couple of weekend after-proms where everyone does their own thing—except their thing is really no different from what thousands of other prom-goers are doing on their after-prom weekend.

Jen, NAHS, North Arlington NJ

After prom everyone drives down to SEASIDE and we drink...and we stay at a hotel for like 3 or 4 days

Sara, Willowbrook HS, Villa Park IL

We're goin' up to my friends' cabin by the dunes for our own little private party and then just chillin' on the beaches the next two days.

Justine, Washington High School, Washington MO

After prom, a bunch of my friends and I are planning on going camping! We are going to go to the campgrounds and hang out, and we might go swimming in the lake! I think it will be so much fun! It sounds really fun! Can't wait!

Cara, Harborfields High School, Greenlawn NY

Honestly, I think me and my friends had the best after-prom ever. Seaside Heights for 3 nights and 2 days...the boardwalk, parties, motel rooms, piercings, beach, pool, food, cops, hospital for alcohol poisoning (haha CraZy Ames!), hot boys, friends...omg it was amazing...I can't wait to go back!

Kelly, Beal Secondary School, London CA
The dance ends at 12am so everyone leaves at about 11pm and they take their limo or drive up to the beach, which is 45 minutes away. My friends have booked this motel so we'll be staying at this place for the weekend and spend the days at the beach (working on our tans) and the nights getting TOTALLY SMASHED!!! :P

Interlude: My Parents

It's hard to know how parents will react to their children—especially the girls—going to prom. The reason is because there are so many misconceptions about what goes on at prom, so many myths. Having these in mind, parents often think the worst—their girl will lose her virginity on prom night because that's what everyone does prom night, right? Their girl will get drunk prom night, because that's what everyone does, right? Worse, she will get drunk in a hotel room—because for some reason, so many parents believe that prom night always ends in a hotel room, with alcohol. Yes, and boys, even long-time boyfriends whom the parents adore at any other time, all turn into wolves.

Not every parent reacts this way when you say the words "prom night." But too many do, especially when it's their daughter's prom and she is being escorted by an upperclassman.

But do teens warrant this kind of reaction? Do they really become irresponsible, drunken, sex-crazed maniacs on prom night? No, of course not—although there's always the exception that likes to ruin it for the rest of us. Most teens have actually learned well from their parents and understand about responsibility and self-restraint. They are much more aware, usually, about their responsibilities and the dangers of sex and alcohol than their parents give them credit for.

In this section, kids speak out about what their parents think of them come prom night. A few want to thank their parents for being supportive. Most, however, are locked in a contest of wills with their parents, and their goal is to be cut a little slack. It's not that they are nearly adult and should be allowed to do whatever they want. This is not what they're saying. It's that they want to have the opportunity to prove to their parents that they can handle themselves and that they understand all about consequences, knowing fully the difference between right and wrong. That is what they are saying.

I never knew how important prom was to parents. My mom in particular. LOL. We have totally bonded over getting me ready for prom. She isn't usually much of a shopper, and she usually doesn't like to spend lots of money if there's a way around it, but she dragged me around the mall, finding the perfect jewelry, bra, slip, etc. I guess it's mostly because my sister wasn't too into prom and didn't tell her she was going until two weeks before, and that didn't give them enough time to prepare. I'm the girly girl in my family, so naturally, I've been looking forward to prom for years! Anyways, girls, if you think including your parents isn't important, think again. It's a really special time for not only you and your date but also for your mom (or even your dad).
(Shelly, New Hope NJ)

I went to my first prom as a freshman. When I tried to confront my mother about my going to prom with my then-boyfriend, who was an 18 yr old senior, I was very afraid she would tell me no, that I was too young. But she didn't do that. She said I could go, but that I couldn't stay out after the prom. I think she said I could go because she never went to her own prom and she was upset that she missed her opportunity and she didn't want me to miss one of mine. This year, my boyfriend and I are both seniors, going to our prom, and my mom is much more relaxed about it, since she has been through it before. She trusts that I won't do anything she wouldn't want me to (for the most part). I have worked very hard to gain her trust, at least the bit that I have, and I wouldn't want to ruin it. This year, she even volunteered to take 9 other ppl and I to the city or other large shopping area so we

could all buy dresses. My mom is pretty OK. My dad doesn't care; he says he was once a boy, he knows what he wanted and what guys want still. None of us listen to him about that anymore though.
(Danielle, Petaluma CA)

Hey all! The first prom I went to was freshman year, and it was sooooo hard to convince my mom to let me go!!! But she finally caved after a few long hours and we went to pick out a dress. They told me to be home by 3 the next morning...right when post prom gets done. I didn't get home until 5! When I walked into the house I was expecting my mom and dad to be waiting up for me, but they had gone to bed!!!! They said they trusted me....nice way to make me feel guilty...lol.
(Sarah, GFC)

My parents tell me my prom night curfew is at 12! Prom ends at 12! How am I to be home before prom is over?! My parents believe that prom night is when all teens have sex! Can they understand that I am eighteen, have been with my boyfriend for 1.5 years, and prom is not just about sex? There are also after parties and clubs and traveling to different places! LOL!
(Alicia, Largo HS, Capital Heights MD)

My parents were a little hesitant when I told them about my post-prom plans. I guess because I was going with someone other than my bf to the dance, but my bf was going to the party with me afterward. I know what you're thinking...that sounds messed up. Well, I am going to the prom with one of my best guy friends. The reason my bf isn't going is because he doesn't know anyone and he can't dance (he has a bad knee). He just wants me to have a good time. The party afterwards is a boy/girl sleep over. So when I told my mother that, she was kinda iffy about it...but after talking to them and assuring them that nothing bad was going to happen, they were okay with it. I gave my rents the number of the girl's mother who's

having the party and they talked for a while about what would be going on…and it went perfectly fine. My parents trust me because I am open and honest about a lot of things. I would really suggest sitting down and talking to your parents in a civil way and try to get them to see your point of view.
(Tara, LC, PA)

When I asked my dad if I could go, he just said, "You're a good girl and I know you'll make good decisions." I was really glad he trusted me that much. Then my mom basically said the same thing, but she added, "You guys are teens and you're gonna do what you want either way, so the best thing we can do is hope you make the right choice."
(Sandra, DCHS, C'ville IL)

My mom is OK about prom. I'm 16 (a sophmore) and my boyfriend is 19 (a senior). My mom is totally against me staying out after prom, which I think is ridiculous because the only reason she can give for not letting me go is my age. But age should have nothing to do with it, it is how you handle yourself in a situation that matters. I really wish she would trust me.
(Alekona, NJ)

My parents don't care (to an extent) about what I do. As long as I tell them the truth and don't lie to them then it's ok. I have four older sisters so I guess by the time they got to me they were a little tired. Actually, last year after prom my parents paid for me, my boyfriend, and some other friends to get a hotel room. They know I'm going to try things, so they would rather know what I'm doing than having me do it behind their backs!
(Bonny, Paoli High School, Paoli OK)

You guys are all on here complaining about how your parents don't trust you…and man, that must suck, because my parents are amazing. They're completely aware of what goes on @

prom, they know we're going to be drinking, but not driving, and they know people will probably be having sex...so they've gone ahead and begun planning a private after-party at our house, so that kids can drink somewhere with supervision. They're amazing, understanding, and remember what it's like to be 18!
(Krissy, London ON)

My parents are definitely iffy on the whole prom idea. Last year was my first year (I was a sophmore...I went with a junior) and I barely convinced them to let me go! They are also concerned that this guy (he lives three hours away) only wants sex and a night of "fun." But to convince my parents otherwise... practically impossible. Thankfully though, they are letting me go again this year with the same guy. So yeah, there isn't a way around your parents, you just have to prove to them that they can trust you with it all.
(Beth, PA)

My parents were really never that concerned about prom night. I went to junior prom for the first time as a sophomore with a guy that I had only been dating a couple weeks, and they were so cool about it. They hardly knew the guy, but that didn't matter to them. I didn't even have a curfew. I'm sure that probably had something to do with the fact that all of my friends were with us and my friends are better at keeping me under control than my parents are. But my senior prom is in a couple months and the parents are letting me spend the entire weekend at an unsupervised house party in Canada. Sure, it's a little dumb of them, but I wouldn't want it any other way. LOL!
(Laura, Grand Island High School, Grand Island NY)

Hey ya'll! I'm a freshman, and I'll be going to a junior/senior prom with my boyfriend who's a junior. He asked me to go, and a couple days later, I said to my mom, "Billy asked me to prom!" To my surprise, she said, "We'd better start looking for a dress!" Some parents are more trusting than others. You just have to work up that trust. It's hard, believe me, I lost it ALL last summer! But I definitely think I'm going to have a hard time convincing my mom to let me go to the after-party at a

hotel. Lol
(Lauren, Fuquay High, Fuquay NC)

My first prom was last year. I was a sophmore going with a junior. I really didn't have a hard time convincing my mom to let me go. I explained to her that he was an athlete and egghead that I really like, and she was happy for me. She let me stay out until 4:30. The trick about staying out late is to just call and check in. I found out that telling the truth to your parents is easier and gets you farther than lying does.
(Jessica, James Logan High School, Union City CA)

I am a junior this year, but since my best friends are seniors, I am going to the senior prom with them. I am going with a group of girls, and we all want to get a hotel room afterwards. Of course, my mom hears the words "hotel room" and immediately thinks the worst. This really irks me, because I may have done stupid things in the past, and I'm the first to admit it, but I'm NOT as bad as she thinks, and our prom night fun will be totally legit. Whatever.
(Chrissa, Burrillville High School, Burrillville RI)

My parents say that they know what all teenagers are up to the night of prom. They told me that they went through the same thing. They told me to have fun but to be careful because there is going to be a lot of drunk drivers. I said how do u know one

of them isn't going to be me? But I told them I was just playing. 'Cause then they wouldn't let me go out after prom. LOL!
(Bianca, Edison High, San Antonio TX)

My parents are very nervous about me going to prom because
they do not know what I am going to do there, so they are very
scared. There is only 2 children in the family, just me and my
brother, and I am the oldest by 2 years. They are scared that
I'm going to go as far as I can on prom night. Prom is the day
after my 17th birthday!!
(Emporia High, Emporia KS)

My parents don't really trust me on prom night. I have a curfew and everything. The thing is, it's totally ironic because my
friends' parents are letting them stay at hotels with their bfs
because they trust them. All my friends are sleeping with their
bfs but their parents are totally oblivious. The funny thing is
that I have really good morals. I'm 17 and have never been
drunk and would never even THINK of doing drugs. Plus I'm
Catholic and I really believe in the whole no sex before marriage thing. My parents think I'm just saying this stuff to gain
their trust. But it's the TOTAL truth!!!! My parents have
almost the perfect child and they don't even know it.
(Cassandra, TX)

This year I am going to the prom as a freshman with my junior
boyfriend (of 1 year) and you might think my parents gave me a
hard time, but they didn't. My mom was completely supportive
of the idea, and we went to purchase the dress as soon as my
date bought the ticket. Spending the night out with my
boyfriend was nothing I was even stressed about. I knew they
wouldn't approve of it, even though they completely love him,
so I didn't even bother asking. If you're put in this situation,

don't complain about it...because THEY CARE ABOUT YOU, all that parents want for you is to be successful and not make bad decisions!! First, gain their respect for you and let them trust you...don't lie about anything...you'll get caught and then what have you accomplished? Then you can party!!!!
(Caitlin, NC)

My best friend and I were both invited to senior prom and we are both juniors. After the prom though, all the seniors were gonna go spend the weekend at a lake house. I knew my mom

wouldn't let me go because my parents are not cool like that. But my best friend was allowed to go and so because my mom knows her and respects her a lot she let me go too. So I guess it really does pay to be friends with people your parents know and respect! LOL.
(Lisa, Houston TX)

I'm a junior and I told my parents that I was going to prom. They said fine, but I have to pay for it. I have no rules or restrictions except for "Respect her." The only thing my parents are giving me is the privilege of driving my mom's brand new Maxima. YEAH! I guess I'm lucky that my parents trust me, but it sucks that so far I've spent about $200 for a tux and corsage, plus another $100 for dinner. Just give your parents a chance, maybe they'll come around.
(Jeff, Hoover High, Birmingham AL)

My parents were totally cool with me going to prom, and camping after that...on top of that they even let me have the car!!!...They trust me, and my friends, they know that we are responsible. They even know that we are drinking, when we get to the campsite...and the only thing my mom said to me was..."be careful!" I thought that was cool. I knew she wouldn't give me a hard time because my older sister went to prom as

well. But for her to give me the car, and know that I would be
drinking was awesome!
(Katrina, St. Bennies, Cambridge ON)

Well, when I was a freshman my then-boyfriend asked me to go
to prom with him at a different school. My dad said I could go,
and that I could sleep at his house, and then go on a weekend
trip with the whole group to go camping. I was really surprised,
cuz that boyfriend was a senior and my father didn't really like
that. I dunno why some parents are totally fine with it and others just won't let it go that you are goin' to go out and do whatever. This year...the last year I am able to go to a prom (sad
:(!)...my father is no longer telling me what to do when prom
comes around. I'll be 18, and he's fine with trusting me. But
those of you who are going...be safe with everything and anything. We are all growing up still and have a few more things to
live for than a drunken prom night that ends in tragedy. Have
a great time and be safe!
(Elizabeth, Lombard IL)

Hey guys, yeah so my senior prom is in 3 days and I told my
dad that we were going camping after with all of my friends.
Then he's like no you're not going and I said what, you expect
me to come home at 12? Um, no. Fine, but if I'm not going
camping I'm staying somewhere else, I'm not going home. But
the prob is EVERYONE is going camping, so there would be
nowhere else to go! It's like the last time all my friends will be
together except for graduation, which I prob can't go to after
parties and stuff bc I'll be with family. But anyways, I am not a
person to do bad things...I don't drink, do drugs, anything.
And my dad still doesn't trust me on going. All of my friends'
parents are letting them go and the only way my boyfriend can
go with me is if it's ok with my dad bc his mom is going to talk
to him about it (make it worse, grrr). So yeah, I don't wanna
be daddy's little girl forever... My grandmother is even ok with

it and my dad doesn't even believe that! O well, I'll see what happens…wish me luck… :-).
(Stephanie, Pilgrim High School, Warwick RI)

My parents think that I am going to get like drunk and guys are going to take advantage of me and everything. I keep telling them that's crap but they won't believe me. Don't you think that parents need more faith in u!?
(Jakki, Rochester NY)

My parents are very strict and I know they care very much about me, but sometimes I feel as though I'll never be able to do anything. I love my parents from the bottom of my heart and I wouldn't want to do anything to hurt them. But I want parents to know, if you tell us not to do something in a loving, careful, respectful way, we'll listen. Just don't try to push your rules in our face. This is a different time and things aren't the same as they were for you. I think parents should lay down the rules but not try to shove them down kids' throats…we get it, already.
(Dont'e, WHS, TX)

Prom has got to be one of the most exciting things in a girl's life. I mean, I love the excitement of getting ready, and then of course when "he" sees you, well there's nothing better than seeing the look on "his" face. It's a hectic time too, worrying about if your dress fits just perfectly, if the hair is in place, and of course if you've popped all those zits that cropped up at the last minute. It always seems to work out just perfectly though.

But the last thing in the world any of us need is our parents freaking out on us. My mother is a prime example of this. Even though she's warned me about sex, rape, and all that other stuff for my whole entire life, she seems to have this crazy idea that I'm suddenly going to forget it all. Now yes, I realize temptation is a huge factor…and that things happen.

But it seems to me, that the more your parents warn you against it, the more the idea is placed in your mind.

When I was asked to the prom, I only thought of the prom, and what we would be doing there. Then my mom says, "Oh, I can just see it now, after the prom you and 'he' will rent a hotel room, or something worse." Do you have any idea how frustrating that is? I mean, with everything else I have to deal with, she comes up with that, and even worse, I remember she mentioned that she might not even let me go. For silly suspicions. And no, there is no reason for her to distrust me...I have been a good child, and worked my tail off for her to let me do things. She's very protective, which is fine, but I think this is taking it too far.

On a good note for her side though, I do understand the fear, the worry, and the not trusting. I'll probably do the same with my children. But I wish she had just kept it to herself, and made me feel like she could really truly trust me.

(Pam, Modesto CA)

EMBARRASSING MOMENTS

Introduction

Prom night is a magical night. Magic—an illusion created by an illusionist. The illusionist's business is to make you believe you have accessed a higher order of reality, an ethereal reality that is somehow better than our regular, everyday world. Does this higher reality exist? That's not the point. The point is that during the performance, you buy into it. But what happens when the magician messes up a trick? Quite suddenly, that magical world collapses and you see through the illusion—you're back in the regular world, if only until the illusionist gets back into the swing of things and takes you up again.

So prom night is a magical night. What the gowns, the tuxedos, the formal setting, the theme and music do is transport you out of your regular, everyday life and into this other universe which is somehow better than the one you just left behind. Again, the point is not whether this higher reality exists. The point is that for that evening, you buy into it.

Until something goes wrong, that is. Until the magician slips up.

And then the magical reality implodes all around you and you are left standing naked (butt naked, in some cases, as you will read) back in the regular world. Of course, we have a word for how you feel at that moment: embarrassed.

It happens to the best of us. Yes, it could happen to you....

I have arranged the 89 stories in the following pages into categories that I think naturally hang together. While lots of odd things happen to prom-goers on prom night, in general, it's the same sorts of things that happen—dresses fall off, boobs fall out, people fart, and so on. Whatever the means, though, these little incidents all inevitably lead up to the collapse of the magical illusion—and to the prom-goer's embarrassment.

A Little Gas

It's a natural thing. It can't be helped. Yet we are taught, even trained, not to do it in public, that it is rude and crude. But we always laugh when we hear the toot. The thing about farting is that presidents and kings do it, and so do you and I. It makes us all human; it anchors us to the regular, everyday world, even when we're all dolled up in our gown and tuxedo finery.

Anonymous
Me and my date went to dinner before the prom and I got a salad with chickpeas and other things. We got to prom and were dancing and dancing and finally it was time to crown the king and queen. My date was called up to be king and then I got called up to be queen. We made our speeches and when we were gonna take a bow, I felt my stomach grumble. We bowed and I let out a fart...the worst part about it was that the microphone was right behind me so it echoed through the whole place....

Jenna, Mesa Verde, Sacramento CA
Alright, this is kind of embarrassing but here goes. So my date is this really hott guy, right? and every girl wants to be the lucky one that gets to go with big ole Franky but I got the cheese, so the night of prom I put my dress on and got all prettied up for his sweet ass and when he got to my house he told me I looked beautiful so I kind of started blushing. Anyway, we got to dinner and (I forgot to mention) I'd had Taco Bell for lunch, so we were just finishing up our meal when I kept getting these slight gassy urges. I kept holding everything in so he wouldn't notice and I thought I was good to go but about 15 minutes later when it was time for dessert the waiter came to ask how every-thing was but he kind of startled me and sure enough (THE BIG BANG!) it was like an explosion. The waiter yelped out OH MY GOD

SHE CRAPPED HERSELF but it was merely a little toot, so everyone
in the place knew I had released my natural gasses and little did we
realize there was a royalty party sitting right behind us and when we
were leaving I noticed. OH MY GOODNESS! They were royalty from
our dance! It was the most humiliating thing in my whole entire
life....

Beth, Atlanta GA

Well, I had been in love with this guy for like 6 years and it was his
senior year in high school, my sophomore year, and I was so stoked
when he asked me to his prom...well...the night finally came and well
I had on a tight beaded dress and well I stood up in the limo to get
something off the floor and I bent over ever-so-cutely...and didn't
know it, but right in his face was my butt...so anyway...about this time
the limo comes to a sudden halt with a jolt and I farted right in my
date's face...but he laughed and we have been dating ever since....

Jaclyn, AL

I actually didn't get asked to prom and I was pretty bummed about it
cuz all my friends did! I was so jealous! I went anyway, hoping that
dateless or not, it would be a blast! And it was...until the song "Dirty"
came on! I was totally excited because it was my favorite song and my
crush Joel came and asked me to dance it with him! I was having such
an awesome time when it happened. He put his hands right on my
butt. I was fine with that, but for some reason I had an extreme
amount of gas that evening, and when he put his hands there I could-
n't help it and I let loose with a loud one! Omg! I was so embarrassed
that I ran right off the dance floor! All my friends were dancing with
their HOTT dates and I had just farted on my crush's hands! Later,
when I thought it was all forgotten about, Joel, who was the MC for
the night, made a total ruin speech about my out-gassing experience!
The whole gym was laughing and staring right at me! I was SO embarrassed! From then on I was known as the gas dancer and no guy wanted to touch my gassy butt ever again!

Guys Embarrassed

Sure, guys get embarrassed—they're human too, you know. So why should we suppose that embarrassment is a girl's thing on prom night? It's just that what embarrasses guys isn't necessarily what embarrasses girls. That's why they're guys and girls are girls.

Caitlin, Weymouth High School, Weymouth MA

Well, my best guy friend had an embarrassing experience last year at junior prom. He had taken his suit jacket off while he was dancing and left it on a chair. When it came time to leave, he picked up his jacket only to find it covered in puke! It stank and all he could do was hold it up and stare at it wide-eyed.

J-Trey, Friendly High School, Fort Washington MD

The night of prom burns my mind to death! The limo picked us up, and halfway there I realized I forgot her flower thingy at home. So we went back and got it and left again and halfway there I realized I had forgotten the tickets in the driveway, so we went back to my house for the second time. When we got to my date's house it was wet outside and I stepped in mud and tracked it in her mom's house on her new white carpet. I was already nervous because her mom, grand-mom, and great-grand-mom were there paparazzi-ing me. Then she came down stairs and it was like a movie. I remember every step. It was a rhythmic thing. My heart pounded and I had butterflies. I'd known this girl for 10 years and had never seen her in a dress until that night. DAMN!!! She was so sexy and beautiful I got even more nervous, so nervous I could only stammer a stupid something or other about how honored I was to be escorting her. Well, after I "calmed" down...I needed to put the flower thingy on her hand but forgot how to do it. So...she did it herself. The whole time I forgot to compliment her on her dress! My mom had to remind me out loud. The picture taking was horrible at her house. They kept saying I looked good...but I wanted out. Later, she refused to dance with me the whole night...and to be a gentleman I stayed with her the whole time, while she was on her cell phone. Then she gave her number out in front of my face to a guy. Then when we got home the limo driver locked me in the car on accident so I couldn't walk her to her door. So now...she attends my college and I'm in love with her...all over again because of prom night... I can't shake these feelings for her. I wish I hadn't been so nervous at prom. J-TREY all the WAY!

Mike, Cardinal Ritter, Indianapolis IN

I was on my way out to the dance floor for a slow dance with my girlfriend. We had just been crowned king and queen so everyone was looking at us. I had on the best tux but my pants were a little too big. So anyway we were slow dancing, and next thing I know everyone is laughing at us. I looked down and the worst thing possible had happened. My pants fell off! It was the worst thing ever because I had on tighty whities. My girlfriend was so embarrassed that she ran away and left me dateless for the rest of the night.

Ryan, Alcona High School, Hubbard Lake MI

I took this very anorexic chick to prom. Dinner cost $35 each and when no one was looking, she threw it on the floor! Then I slipped on her twice-baked potato. I fell and dropped my tropical delight all over my $200 tux! Then when dessert came around, she was in the bathroom barfing! Don't know whether I was more embarrassed or pissed off!

Randy, IA

Well this really hot girl who I'd been totally crushing on asked me to the formal and I was totally psyched, man, you know. I was just soooo happy. Anyway, I bought this powder blue tuxedo (it sounds corny but I looked really hott!) and hired a limo. Anyway, we went to dinner, then when we got to the prom we danced and stuff and had a really great time. We were lucky enough to be made king and queen and went up on stage to collect our awards. All of a sudden everyone started hollering and laughing at me. At first I didn't know what was happening, but then I looked down and much to my disgust there was a big dark blue stain on my crotch, which had probably been there since dinner. I never went back to school after that and my date never spoke to me again.

Weirdos

It's probably no accident that the people doing weird things in these stories are all guys. Don't know why, but guys are more prone than girls to deliberately ruining the magic. I can't imagine a girl showing up to her prom in a Superwoman outfit. But guys....

Heather, Rim of the World, Crestline CA

OK, my boyfriend and I are going to prom. I'm wearing this sexy red dress that I designed myself and he's wearing a matching zoot suit that I also designed. We tried them on at the dressmakers together the day before prom and we looked hot!!! Well, he calls me while I'm getting my hair done the next day and tells me his suit has disappeared. He says not to worry, and prom night he shows up in a Superman outfit!!! His idea of a joke....

Jesika, Florien High, Florien LA

I was in the tenth grade going to my first prom ever with a senior. First, he showed up at my house in a lime green tuxedo and his friend in a baby blue one (I guess to copy *Dumb and Dumber*). I was hoping to boost my popularity by going with him, but I don't guess that will happen. Second, I wore a white dress but I couldn't wear panties because it would show. Everyone was laughing at us when we walked in, but after our first dance they were laughing hysterically. I guess my date needed some reassurance in his manhood because half way through the dance whatever was in his pants busted (I guess it was water) and got all over both of us. When I pulled away from him to see what it was, I noticed you could see straight through my dress and so could everyone else. Needless to say, after that I was known as Playboy bunny in training!

Jen, Cohasset High School, Cohasset MA

I was at my senior prom and everything was going fine until my date showed up wearing a really weird suit that was bright blue with ugly red shoes.

Melanie

Our prom had really blown ass, so a couple of friends and I went to see a few guys at another friend's house. When we got there we were all wet cuz it had been raining really hard. The guys thought that was really funny, so they started prancing around singing love songs. When we finally decided to leave, two of the guys walked us home but they threw worms down our dresses. So there we were, two completely soaked girls with worms wiggling their way down our dresses. It was so gross!!!

Kristi, Michigan City High School, Michigan City IN

It was the night of prom my senior year. Well my date decided to be really funny and I didn't know it but after we got to the prom he went to the bathroom and when I saw him again he'd come out naked.

Christina, Colonial Heights High, Colonial Heights VA

Oh my gosh! Well just a couple weeks before my prom, my dad made me break up with my boyfriend of a year and a half!! So I had no date!! My friends hooked me up with one of their friends and I didn't meet him until that night...when he showed up with a full COW PRINT TUX!!! How embarrassing is that? The whole night I danced with friends and only ended up dancing with him during two slow songs. It was horrible!

Leeann, Marion High School, Marion, IL

I went to prom my freshman year with my best friend's cousin, and when we got there I was embarrassed to dance with him because, well, he wasn't very good at it...at all. So when I danced the first slow dance with a friend instead of him, he got really upset, and did not come dance again but stared at me while I had fun for the rest of the night. He wouldn't move from the seat. He sat there at our table and tore up our camera, then the napkins, and finally shredded the tablecloth...how weird is that? Then when it was time for after-prom, I was going out to his car to cheer him up, but as I passed the dance floor, I looked down and saw my change of clothes thrown all over the floor...which included my bra and panties.

Derek, Meadville PA

i know that i'm a guy but hey i have prom stories also. i wore a kilt to prom last year. i was just sitting back and enjoying the night. i was voted most original tux. and when i got up to go out to the dance floor to dance with my gorgeous date i hadn't known that the boys had played a bit of a prank on me. they had taken off my brooch pin and untied my belt. being odd on my own i wasn't wearing anything underneath. they had tied my kilt to the back of my chair also. so if you are of any intellegence you know what happened next. i got up. and i was moving pretty fast. i kind of made it clear out to the dance floor before i knew what happened. the people watching us didn't listen when i said it wasn't my fault so i got kicked out of my own prom. i loved every minute of it. but hey i didn't drive, i had to wait for my best friend to come out. he didn't know that i got kicked out since he was way too enthused by his date's dress. so i waited outside until midnight when prom ended. on top of everything. i lost my date to my worst enemy. she said i was too weird. so i just went home that night. looking back on it. it was my best prom ever.

Slips and Spills

Couple of things happening here. People slipping. Or people spilling. And sometimes both: people spilling because they're slipping. This may be the most common source of embarrassment at prom, and the most natural anywhere. It's expected that you will get a little punch on yourself or miss a step as you stride gracefully across the ballroom. Of course, having the punch bowl hurled at you or rolling down the stairs with your entire prom committee—that's something else altogether.

Tina, Newark Valley High School, Newark Valley NY

It was last year's prom, and we had really bad weather. When we got to the prom it had just stopped raining. My date was really nice and offered to carry me to the door so my white shoes and dress wouldn't get wet and muddy. Just as we were getting to the door, my date lost his balance and fell, throwing me into a huge mud puddle. I was soaked head to toe and my dress became see through when it was wet. Then everyone got to see the sexy underwear I was wearing for my date for after prom. I was so mortified.

Anon

My freshman year I got asked to prom by one of my friends. It was his senior prom so he went all out, renting a limo, buying me jewelry and all. So it's prom night and the night was going well. Then we all were called together to parade down the grand staircase at the hotel to show off our gowns to about 2000 waiting friends and parents. Wouldn't you know it, I slipped on one of the steps and fell down the stairs dragging my date with me. I felt like a total loser! We fell for like twenty steps, mostly on our butts, and everyone was screaming and jumping out of our way. I was mortified, but later, my date assured me that it was cool and that at least we were memorable. This made me feel better, especially since Monday at school people taunted me with homemade videos that had captured our spill. He still promised me that there was no girl that could have made a better prom date. So now I am going to make it my tradition to tumble down the stairs every year just to make a splash and have some alternative fun. I'm glad his senior prom wasn't traditional—as he had expected—because, hey, I'm not exactly a traditional girl, and I think that makes me all the more beautiful.

P.S. This year I'm being taken to the prom by my boyfriend of 9 months. We plan to tumble down the stairs TOGETHER!

Dawn, Ann Arbor MI
I slipped on the edge of the limo as I was getting out and I fell face first in a puddle.

Brandi, Gore High School, Gore OK
We arrived at prom and as I walked in and everyone was looking at me I tripped and fell flat on my face. That was embarrassing....

Paige, Kansas
I bought a killer dress. It fit me very well and gave me great cleavage. Well when I got to the prom I tripped on my dress and bumped into this guy that was really hott and his ice cream went down my great cleavage. It was so embarrassing.

Germaine, Mayflower Secondary, S'pore
Our school was holding a buffet-style dinner instead of a la carte. I bent down at the buffet table to smell the barbequed chicken when out of the blue this guy, who was being pushed around by his friends, fell onto me, knocking me over onto the floor. "BUMMER!" I was so amazed that it took me about 10 seconds to realize a guy was sitting on me, his butt on my crotch. He got up and left, but came back a few minutes later to apologize. I was holding a glass of sparkling wine and

talking to him when my friend went up to me and patted me on the back. I jumped, and my wine went all over him.

Marsha, Malley High, Dallas TX

Well it was so embarrassing. I had this perfect pink dress. I looked beautiful. Well when my date came he looked so hott. We went to prom and I got voted prom queen. I was walking down the steps with my crown on, tripped, and went rolling down and onto the floor. To make things worse, my dress fell completely off and everyone was laughing!!!

Debra, MS

Well, it was my senior prom, and I was so excited because I'd never been to prom before, and I'd looked forward to this night all of high school.

I got my dress; it was so pretty; it was a white strapless dress, and since I didn't have a strapless bra I decided to just not wear one.

I was going with the most popular guy in school. He was so HOTT!! Anyways, it was cool because prom was on a cruise ship (the Natchez), and we got on it and me and my date got on the deck of the ship, and I was pretending to fly (like on *Titanic*). Well then my date decided to tickle me (dumbass! :)), and I went flying all right, right over the side of the boat. It really sucked because I am afraid of water and can't swim. Everyone heard the splash and they had to throw a life-preserver out to me, and my principal had to jump in to save me. He pulled me back onto the boat, and I was completely drenched. On top of all that my soaked dress was totally see-through now and you could see everything (including my polka dot thong). What's worse is that because we were on a boat, I couldn't leave until we were back at the dock, three hours later. It was the worst night of my life.

My date was sweet though, and he gave me his jacket to cover up in, and he stayed by me all night long. We ended up hooking up later that week! :)

Allison, Northern Heights, Los Angeles CA

It was prom night and I was part of the planning committee and we had done an awesome job planning out the whole evening. We were getting recognized for putting the whole thing together and we had to go up on stage. As I was walking up I tripped on the stairs and I took down four other girls with me! Not only that, but one of the girls completely toppled over, exposing to all that she decided NOT to wear any underwear that night. The whole committee never lived it down.

Sandra, Beverly Hills High, Beverly Hills PA

So I had this white dress that was like the hottest thing I have ever seen cuz it was almost nonexistent and my bf LOVED it cuz of that...but anyways...we showed up at prom and everyone was complimenting us cuz we were like sooooooo cool! and they obviously wanted to be associated with us...but not by the end of the night lol! So we went to get a drink and the drinks had those little umbrellas in them and my boyfriend tripped and accidentally spilled the drink (which was of course red lol) all over my dress (which used to be white lol) and then he fell on me and the little umbrella poked through my water bra so I was majorly uneven the rest of the night. It was sooooooo embarrassing it was like the worst thing I have ever experienced!

The Whole Dress Goes Whoosh!

This is probably the worst that could happen. It's not only that your whole dress comes off, leaving you either entirely naked or in bra and panties. It's also the illusion of the evening, the magic, that is stripped from you. And finally, your dignity is also stripped from you, because it's very hard to maintain a dignified appearance when you are standing butt-naked in a crowded place. You've all heard about people dreaming those dreams in which they are in a room full of fully dressed people, but they are naked. Well, here's that dream come true!

Jen, Melbourne FL

I was at the prom and I looked gorgeous! I was wearing a long strapless red silk dress (it fit snug and perfect!) and matching red stilettos (the heels were tiny!!!) Well I was walking on a wooden bridge and my heel got stuck in a tiny hole in the bridge. While I was trying to get my heel out of the hole, my heel broke and I fell on my butt and my left boob popped out. But right as I was putting my boob back in my (strapless) dress, my totally hott boyfriend came by to help me up and neither of us noticed that he was standing on my dress and when he pulled me up my dress ripped all the way up revealing my pink see-through thong and matching strapless bra! My boyfriend immediately gave me his jacket and drove me home. I cried the whole way home and for the next 3 days I wasn't embarrassed, I was mortified.

P.S. My boyfriend felt so bad about ripping my dress and humiliating me in front of the whole school that he paid me for the dress and took me out to dinner.

Kristy

Alright, it was prom night and I was wearing a new tight white strapless dress. I had also bought some new lingerie. My date and I had been dancing for a few songs and then we walked to where the drinks were. On the way over, the bottom of my tight dress got caught on a nail sticking out of the edge of the door and because everyone was coming out at this time through this one door, I couldn't stop. I was being pushed and so my dress just RIPPED STRAIGHT OFF!!! By the time everyone had stopped moving I was about 300 feet away from my dress, which was still hanging on the nail. I was standing there in the middle of about 500 people wearing nothing but a completely SEE THROUGH G-STRING AND LACY BLACK SUSPENDERS. My boobs were hanging out and I was practically NAKED!!!! To make it worse some geek ran off with my dress!!!!

Katie, Baltimore MD

OK, my date and I were on our way to my senior prom in a stretch limo. It was raining pretty hard. I had spent 2 hours doing my hair and I didn't want it messed up. When we got there, the driver got out, walked around to the back, and opened the door for us. My date got out first and then he took my hand and helped me out. We wanted to hurry to get out of the rain so as soon as we stepped out of the car, we began to run for the door. I don't think the driver was paying attention to what he was doing because he closed the door on my dress. The dress was made of really light material and when I stepped away from the car, I felt something pulling on me and then a ripppppp! My date didn't realize anything was happening and kept pulling me by the hand toward the door. Next thing I know, I'm being pulled through the rain wearing only a white pushup bra, a very short white lacy slip, white panties, off-white thigh highs and white heels! I screamed at my date to stop. I ran back to the car to get my dress but the door was locked. In his haste to get out and open our door, the driver had locked the keys in the car! The dress was ruined and there wasn't much I could do with it anyway, so I said the hell with it. My date and I went in without it. I spent the first hour of the prom walking around in just my bra and slip until my mom brought me my gown from my junior prom. Luckily, I went to a private school and most everyone there was understanding and didn't make a big deal about it.

Laura, Sheldon Heath Community School, Birmingham AL

I went to the prom looking the best and I went to the punch table to get myself a drink and spilt some on the floor and when I bent down to clean it up my dress split and came right off because it was two sizes too small (I'm a bit overweight). Everyone was laughing!

Jenny, Greenville High School, Greenville ME

I bought a nice strapless gown for my prom but it needed to be taken in so I took it to a seamstress. What I didn't know was that the person doing the alterations on my dress was my biggest rival's sister. So my rival herself sneaks into the shop one night and loosens all the seams on my gown. Come prom night and I'm dancing with my date. I start to feel something strange happening with my gown. It's getting all crinkly and loose feeling, and right before my eyes it starts to come apart at the seams. The more I move the faster it opens—and it's opening everywhere. I start to head for the bathroom when my rival comes up behind me and steps on my train and off comes my dress. There I am in the middle of the dance floor totally humiliated in my thigh highs and strapless bra and thong! And I can't even put the dress back on because it's in about four pieces! Everyone starts laughing at me as I try to cover up and I just run out of there. That's one night I'll never forget!

Britney, Palm Beach FL

Well you know how everyone wears long dresses to prom. Well I wore a short red one. And I'm talking short. It was just one cm away from my butt! Well I have a killer body and when my boyfriend picked me up he accidentally ripped the back on my dress, which was strapless. After the prom we all played blind man's bluff in the auditorium. It was my turn and I was on the stage alone and everyone was watching me trying to catch someone...I was blind folded. I don't know how, but I popped out of my dress, and I was standing there onstage with only a thong and a bra. And the worst thing is I didn't even notice! The people all took photos!

aLL TiMe LoSeR, SoMeWhere

OK, so I just started high school (freshman) and I meet this really awesome guy. He's a senior. He asks me if I want to go to his prom with him and I'm like omg sure because I love proms. Anyway, I have to find a really special dress because I want to be totally different from everyone else. So I ask my grandma if she could make one for me because she's all awesome with that. So she says yea sure, we'll make it pretty and blah blah blah....Anyway, she makes this awesome puffy white dress...it looks like a wedding dress...it's sooo awesome. So my date comes and picks me up in the limo...totally romantic...flowers...music...you know, the whole deal. We get to prom and go in and the principal is there saying hi and filming everyone as they walk up....let me tell you....So whatever, everything is all cool when all of a sudden I feel a little pop on my back....Now I'm like, omg....I run to the bathroom and one of my friends happens to be in there and I tell her about the pop and she says my zipper just broke. So I had to safety pin my dress back together, which turned out OK...until I got to the dance floor and started grinding with my boyfriend....Well lets just say my safety pins opened...and so did my dress....I was like, omg, my dress is on the floor....I didn't know what to do...total bummer....

Butt Showing

This is a lot like the whole dress going whoosh, except that it's only a partial whoosh—just enough to put a kink in the magical reality of your evening, without entirely collapsing the illusion.

Sam, Manasquan High School, Belmar NJ

My dress was a really cute two-piece, but tight fitting, especially around my butt. When I stepped out of the limo my heel got caught on the bottom of my dress and pulled it down. My thong was completely showing so I started to run for cover and someone screamed, "YOU HAVE A FLABBY ASS!!"

Nikki, Refugio High School, Refugio TX

It was my freshman year and the guy of my dreams asked me to prom. I bought the most expensive and sexiest dress of them all. It was a little snug, but it was so pretty, and the only one, so I had to get it anyway, although I couldn't breath in it. So the night comes, and my date picks me up in a limo and we arrive at prom. As we are getting out of the limo, I hear a rip. I stop and suddenly realize it was my tight dress, that it had ripped all the way down. It was so embarrassing, and the guy of my dreams was right behind me. He saw everything, everything! And I had decided not to wear a bra or panties that night. So he saw it all. I cried the whole night and asked the limo driver to take me home.

Anonymous

My boyfriend and I got to prom and went out on the dance floor to do a little grinding. We were having a great time and danced non-stop almost all night. We even got to take our pictures with our friends. I had a hot pink faded dress; it was strapless and extremely short. Near the end of the prom we were still dancing when I noticed that everyone was cheering me on. I didn't quite understand why when I was only dancing with my friends. At that moment my boyfriend pulled me from the dance floor and dragged me toward the exit. As I began to ask why he was making a scene, he spun me around and pulled down the bottom of my dress. That's when I realized that as I was dancing, I had gone down a little too low, and now the bottom of my dress was like up around my hips. It was so embarrassing that my boyfriend told me he was glad we didn't have to go to another prom night.

Kayla, Jackson MS

It was my senior prom. I had a beautiful dress; it was a pink two-piece. My date and I went to get our pictures taken. Well, neither of us knew it, but my date was standing on my dress when I decided to change my pose. I turned the other way and my entire skirt came off. I was left squatting on the floor with granny panties on and my top. I was sooooooo embarrassed and I cried the whole month. But after that people let it go. THANK GOD!!!!!!

Anonymous, VT

I was walking and I didn't want my dress to drag in the dirt so I lifted it and I had totally forgotten that I had a slit up the back of my dress and I lifted it too far and I was wearing a thong and everyone saw my butt!

Boobs Out

This too is a lot like the whole dress going whoosh, only this time, it's the upper half—also just enough to be disturbing, perhaps creating a ripple or two in the magical reality of prom night.

Anonymous, Toronto ON

Dis was at senior prom...i went wid my date...he's nice n all...but there was dis guy i had the biggest crush on...and there he was...n he looked soooo good...cudnt take my eyes off him...so i take out my camera to take his picture hoping he wudnt see me...coz we werent exactly talking to each other...well i move in closer without my date...my girlfriend helped me move with my strapless dress n all...n i finally get the courage to aim n shoot...n finally when i put the camera down i notice him lookin at me...n i was scared he was gonna be really mad at me...he came closer n said "do u alwayz take pics by showing"...n to my horror i realize my dress has slid down n my braless boobs were popping out...i was so embarrassed...i ran to the washroom wid my girlfriend...but when i came out he was standing rite at the door asking if i was alrite...i guess it helped us become friends... :-)

Jess, JCHS, KY

It was my senior prom and I was standing around with a couple of friends when all of a sudden I looked over to see this somewhat chunky girl whose boob was hanging out! I guess it was wrong but I screamed at her because obviously she hadn't noticed. Hey! I'd want someone to tell me if my boob popped out!

Karee, New York NY

OK it was my prom and I was going with this really hott guy. He was fine!!! Well like one week before the prom I was so nervous I couldn't eat and I didn't really want to eat either so I would look good. Well we went out to eat and I still didn't eat much...but when we got to the dance I kept on having to pull my strapless dress up 'cause it kept falling down. Then when I was dancing with my date my dress fell almost all the way down 'cause I had lost so much weight in the last week that it was too big!!!!! I picked it up and ran to the bathroom. I was SO embarrassed!!

Ann, Palm Creek North, Los Angeles CA

Alright, it was the night of prom and I had never been more excited in my life! My dress was gorgeous, my hair was perfect, and my boyfriend looked amazing. Well, after dancing for a while we decided to get our picture taken, and so the photographer positioned us in a cute pose with my boyfriend's arms around me. Right when he was taking the picture my boyfriend sneezed and knocked me forward and my boobs came right out of my strapless dress!! I really hope they don't develop the film or my mom and dad will kill me!!

Cold Cut, Central High School, Philadelphia PA

Well it was my senior prom. Everything was great, my date, my dress, hair, etc....When we first walked in we went to take pictures but I didn't know my dress was falling apart, so as I posed for the picture my dress fell down and I was left sitting there topless. I ran out screaming, I was so embarrassed. What made it even worse is they had pictures!

Anonymous

Well, it was my first prom and I was a freshman going with my boyfriend who's a junior. Seeing how I really didn't know how the whole prom thing went I was really nervous, especially since none of my friends were going. Anyway, my boyfriend drove us in his dad's old Mustang pace car and everything was going really really well and I was soooo happy that nothing bad or embarrassing had happened...but I spoke too soon. It was the last dance (slow dance) so EVERYONE was on the dance floor, and me and my boyfriend were dancing really close and he had his hands on my back right near my zipper. Well I guess he thought I had something on my dress and he pulled on it, but what he really was pulling was my zipper! My dress was strapless and was really tight so I didn't notice until the song was over and we started to walk back to our table and my dress fell enough for my boobs to pop out...with no bra on! Luckily I have a funny one for my boyfriend. He found it hilarious and laughed...but then of course the sweet side took over and he helped me zip back up :) But how embarrassing, right? Next time I'm definitely wearing a strap-less bra!

Katie, USC, Wells MN

It was prom night and my date came to my house to pick me up in his pickup. I got in and we went to the school. When I was getting out of the truck my flowers fell on the ground, and when I bent down to get them my boobs popped out. And when I went to stand up my heel caught on the back of my dress and my dress ripped open. So my boyfriend got some duct tape and taped the dress back together. I went to the prom alright, but I didn't go to school the rest of the week.

Kimberly, Watkins Memorial, Pataskala OH

My friends and I had rented a limo for prom and one of the other girls and I were really hyper. Every time the limo stopped, we'd lean out the windows and do silly things like ask people if they had any Grey Poupon mustard. When we got to the dance, we saw another of our friends, so I leaned out to say "hi." I really hadn't been thinking the whole time, but my dress was very low cut and when I leaned over you could see everything. My chemistry teacher, who was male, happened to be standing right outside the limo window with a video camera. So, my teacher got a wonderful view of me...and to make matters worse, for the rest of the year, he was really, really nice and started giving me higher grades than everyone else for the same work. I still haven't lived it down.

Mikaela, Seattle WA

My senior prom was so embarrassing. I had bought this super low-cut dress that revealed almost everything. A couple of my friends told me I should try this double-sided tape to keep the dress in place, but I thought I'd be OK 'cause the dress didn't feel like it would move or slide down. My boyfriend picked me up in his car, and everything was going great. When we got to prom, we danced and all that forever. They announced the winner for prom queen and it was me! I made it to the top of the stage OK, but when I bent over so they could put my crown on, my boobs fell out of my dress. The crowd went silent, and then they all started laughing. There's even a picture in my yearbook where they had to block out my boobs. My boyfriend was the only good part, because when I had left the stage this guy tried to pull the top of my dress aside to "get another look" and my boyfriend beat the crap out of him.

Noelle, Manasquan HS, Avon NJ

I had specially picked out this tight fitting dress that showed my cleavage for my date. The dress had sequins at the top and was very uncomfortable...it irritated me sooo much! We went to dinner with his friends and all through the meal I was fidgeting with it and pulling it this way and that. I went to the bathroom to adjust it some more and when I was returning, and still inching down my top, I wasn't paying attention to the waiter in front of me. I ran right into him, yet I kept walking. Little did I know, but the accident with the waiter had left my nipple hanging out. Before I knew it, my boyfriend and his jerky friends were all laughing at me. It was the worst night ever!! :(From then on they called me "FIRE NIPPLE!" because the sequins had scratched me all up and my nipple was red and irritated.

Megan, in Hell

Yeah, well, it was prom and I didn't want to go. My best guy friend asked me though, so I couldn't say no and I'm like, OK. So I do the whole dress-up bit and I get a pretty strapless dress and we go. And we're there and me n him and some other ppl get in a mosh pit and sumI steps on my dress and boing, my boobs pop out, eeeee! Well my date grabbed me so no one would see and gave me his jacket and I ran to the bathroom. He was so sweet about it but I was really, really embarrassed.

Boob Troubles

Since this isn't really about boobs coming out, but about, ahem, enhancements, I thought it deserved a short chapter of its own.

Kelly, Northwest High School, KS

Okay, so it was my very first prom right? And I was so excited. I had to get the perfect dress and everything. So I found one and it was so incredibly great...the only problem was my boobs weren't big enough for it. So no big deal. I got some of those little jelly cup things. And when I was dancing on the floor with my date, my dress started to slip down and you could see the cup. What made it even worse is that some girl came up and began poking at it! I ran to the bathroom crying....Moral: NEVER GET FAKE BOOBS!!!

Rebecca, St. Marks, Ottawa ON

Well I had my dress on but the part for my boobs didn't quite fit properly, it was a little too big. So I just figured I could stuff some Kleenex in there to make it bigger. When my hott date and I were dancing the Kleenex just happened to fall out. Everyone saw what I had done and my date looked at me and said, "Those weren't real." I was so embarrassed that I ran into the bathroom and didn't come out for like ten songs!!

Hair Off

Hair is a big deal on prom night, and girls spend hours getting it just right. It's a major contributor to the illusion of an ethereal reality greater than the mundane, so when the hairpiece comes off, or all of it falls out, whoooom, there goes your reality.

Becky, Jersey Shore Senior High School, Jersey Shore PA

Last year before the prom I had just gotten my hair cut too short to pull up so I had my stylist put a hairpiece on the back and curl it. Everything was going great and even my hair looked natural. My boyfriend and I were having a great time dancing and then a slow song came on and the night got even better. Until...my boyfriend's favorite song came on and he got really excited and ripped his hands off me. Along with his arms came my hairpiece—it was stuck in his cuff link. Everyone was around us and laughing hysterically. It was so embarrassing but I had to laugh because I am such a dork for even getting a hairpiece. This year I will go all-natural.

Christina, Sacramento CA

My girlfriends and I were without dates for the prom so we decided to do each other's hair for fun. We were running late and decided to finish mine in the bathroom at the prom. As upset as I was because of this I had to agree. So I had to go to the prom with a shower cap on while the concoction of "deep conditioners" set in. While that may seem embarrassing, we were able to slip into a side door at the hotel, relatively unnoticed.

We got into the bathroom and my friend Cindy was going to rinse my hair in the sink, blow dry it with the travel blow dryer, and brush it out. That is where the horror started. As soon as she started rinsing it, my hair began falling out in large clumps. I freaked out and fainted, but luckily Cindy caught me. I was crying uncontrollably as she rinsed off the rest of the "conditioner" leaving me completely bald. It turned out that Cindy's mom had been keeping a hair remover gel in a bottle Cindy thought was a deep conditioning product!

I've never been so humiliated as other girls came into the bathroom and saw my shiny bald head. Cindy ushered me through the gathering crowd and out to the car. Everyone who saw me was laughing at the bald girl in the prom dress. I cried for days after that, but my mom got me a wig so I could at least go outside, and I had to finish the school year wearing a wig, too.

The Dress Does Not Fit

Not too large, no. Always too small. Always, always too small. Why is that, girls?

Angela, Cherry Hill NJ

I picked out my dress really early (around Thanksgiving) and got a great deal on it. Unfortunately, I got a little piggy and gained about 30 pounds by the prom. I managed to squeeze myself into the dress but at dinner the zipper ripped open and I had to go home and change. I should have ordered a salad!

Jocelyn, Howard PA

It was the night of my junior prom and I was really excited. I have what doctors call a little bit of a weight problem. I may be chubby but I don't care—I flaunt it with the best of them. I found this beautiful strapless dress with a slit up the side. My mom said that the slit was a little high but I didn't care. Well I get to the prom and all is well 'cause you can't tell about my "weight problem." The hottest guy, I mean, that one guy that you've been in love with forever and never thought you could have, came over and told me how nice I looked— and it was like my dream come true. Well we started dancing and were having the time of our life when I felt someone step on my dress and as I turned around I heard this giant rip. The dress was now slit up to just below my chest. Being the nutcase that I am I just continued to dance when all of a sudden I hear one of my teachers speaking over the microphone and she's calling my name and asking me if I would leave because my fat was hanging out. I was sooo embarrassed!!!

Steph, SHS, NJ

I was getting ready with my friend and we were getting our dresses on.

I had bought mine over the summer. So I went to put it over my head and it got stuck! I couldn't get it on anymore, and I couldn't get it off! I started yelling for my friend to help me. She pulled and it didn't budge. She pushed and I finally got it off me. I started to panic even more because I didn't have another dress and I kept saying, "I didn't think I got that fat over the summer? Oh my gosh I gained weight! Oh my gosh! What am I going to do!?" But at the end of it all we found out that I hadn't unzipped the dress all the way! Can you say "blonde!" Wow!!

Beverly, Montgomery AL

I wanted to wear a slinky tight bias cut evening gown but I was not in tiptop shape so I looked kinda bulgy. I thought a shaper might help and Mom took me to a small shop where they custom fit you for like girdles. I tried several on with the dress and finally bought something called a "long leg panty corselet." It was horribly uncomfortable but I thought it would loosen up or stretch or something after a while. Well, I bought the corselet two months before prom and I didn't try it on again until prom night. That was a big mistake! I just managed to get it on, and I looked great, but I could hardly move in it, it was so stiff.

That night my date kept asking me if I was alright because I was just kinda standing around and trying to hold in my breath so I wouldn't feel so cramped. So I told him yes, and I blamed it on my dress. Well, as soon as we slow danced he figured it out. He began teasing me, and then he told other people what I was wearing. Like that wasn't bad enough, I went to the bathroom and after I was finished I couldn't close it up again. I spent like an hour in there and finally I gave up and took it off. I felt bad because my mother had bought it and it had cost a lot, but I just left it in the bathroom.

Well my story doesn't end there because I hadn't been with my boyfriend ten minutes, and he still hadn't let me live down the corselet thing, when one of my friends suddenly dances by with my corselet on the end of a stick, like a flag. Everybody was laughing and to this day I haven't lived it down!

Moral: Don't wear a corselet. And if you must, then get it the night before prom.

Periods

Prom, whether by theme or just in the way people dress for the evening, strives to be otherworldly, ethereal, magical. I've said this a few times now, I know. Still, what more powerful way to be reminded of the mundane than the onset of one's period?

Christina, O'Leary High School, Edmonton AB

The day of grad I got my period, and it was super heavy. I had not expected it, and I had no tampons in my purse. My friend happened to have a fat pad, which I took, but I was wearing a thong so it wasn't very secure. So...I was nominated prom queen. I was so astonished! When I walked up to get my crown, my pad fell onto the stage in front of the whole school. I didn't notice, and neither did the prom king as he came onto the stage and stepped on it. He suddenly slipped, hitting the stage face first and breaking his nose. I was so embarrasssssed!!!

Sarah, Denker High, Denker CT

I was wearing this really sexy white dress and I had just had my period. I thought it was over so I was really happy. Me and my date (this really hott guy) were sitting down during one song drinking punch. When I got up my friends started laughing cuz I had a HUGE red spot on my butt. I thought it was my period and I ran to the bathroom. My friends came in after me and told me I was sitting in punch. I was relieved but MORTIFIED!

Sammy, Bensalem High School, Philadelphia PA

i was getting ready for my prom like 2 hours and i had a stain on my bed that i didn't c i put my off-white prom dress on my bed for 5 min cuz i was doin my nails then i came back and put my dress on i didn't

know that there was a stain on my dress everything i thought was perfect until i arrived at the prom my date was even embarrassed to come
in with me so he said wait outside for a sec then I realized it was gettin
like 15 min and he still didn't show up so i went then EVERYONE i
mean EVERYONE was staring at me then my friend ran up to me and
put his jacket around my waist and i said y r u doin that he asked me if
i got my period i slapped him i thought that it was a personal question
he said no no blood is all over the back of your dress i screamed and
he was so sweet he took me home i got changed put on some sweats
and we went back to the prom and had a blast. Now we are happily
married with 3 kids.

Mistaken

Sometimes the magician makes a little error when he's showing us the magic reality. A wrong move, the wrong words, an improperly closed magic box. In short, a little mistake. But that one little mistake changes everything.

Embarrassed, Holston High School, Damascus VA

I was waiting for my date to get to my house the night of the prom and he never showed up...I was sooo sad I missed my first prom! I was more mad than sad though so the next day I saw my "date" and said where were you I was waiting for you all night and he said that he went to the address I gave him and an old lady answered the door and called him a pervert! He showed me the paper that I had written my address on and I had made a mistake and put 77120 instead of 77210...he hasn't talked to me since!! :(OOPS

Marie, La Mirada High School, La Mirada CA

At our prom we had shout-outs for a couple of dollars. You write a note to someone and the DJ reads it out loud. Well there is this girl who has the same name as me. She wrote this long emotional letter confessing her love to this guy she had liked for four years. Well after she turned it in she got so embarrassed she left before it was read. Well she had only signed her first name (remember, we have the same first name) so when the DJ read it everyone thought I HAD WRITTEN IT! I was so embarrassed!

Cammie and Camille, That place that we go to when Mom and Dad make us, PA

Well, it all started two weeks before prom. My twin sister (Camille) and I had bought similar dresses. Hers was a leopard print halter-top and mine was a zebra print halter-top. We each had dates that were equally good looking. They had decided to pick us up at our house and then we'd share the limo and do all that sorta stuff together. Her date kept calling me Camille and mine kept calling her Cammie. The only way to tell us apart was the print of the dress. When we finally got to the hotel (our school holds prom at a hotel...it makes it easier) we decided to dance. Well it was dark and you really couldn't tell what the dress looked like. This guy comes up behind me, grabs my butt, and says did your butt get smaller?? I turn around and see Camille's date standing there. He thought I was her (and still did at this point), and she came over but refused to talk to either of us—me for having the better butt, and him for grabbing it. My own date was completely shocked and wouldn't talk to me for a week, until he finally broke down and let me explain it to him. Camille and I have decided our butts are equally fabulous!

Jackie, Alden High School, Bangor ME

At my prom I was with the guy of my dreams, just a total hottie, and it was going to be THEE night of the year, maybe of my life. And of course, right before the prom, I got my period, wouldn't you know! So I was all worried about how that was going to affect my prom and was hoping it wouldn't. All went well most of the night, no cramps, no problems, and then right at the evening's end when they were going to announce the king and queen, and my date and I were up near the front, my friend Angie comes up behind me and whispers, "Jackie, red stain on the back of your dress!" And I thought, OMG, this is just great!" and began to blush big time. Well I was trying to make a subtle exit to the bathroom when the guy next to my own date gets picked prom king and the spotlight comes on and illuminates me and my date and the other people near the new king, and of course everyone's looking our way and I want to slide right through the floor at that moment. So I go, "Angie, cover me! Quick!" And Angie goes, "How come?" And I said, "The stain on the back of my dress?????" And she says, "Huh? NOOOO! I said 'Fred Stine on the back of your dress!' The Fred Stine designer tag is showing! THAT'S what I said!"

Angie, bless her bones, never let me live THAT misunderstanding down!

The Animals' Fault

Sometimes, it really isn't the magician's fault that the illusion collapses. Maybe the rabbit doesn't want to pop out of the hat. Or maybe the horse does.

Brin, Loserville High School, Toronto ON

It was the perfect night and I had on a long dress that was very puffy. So I kinda looked chunky! Well, my date arrived and we went to the prom in a horse and buggy. We had planned it to be the perfect nite until we got out of the buggy and the horse had to go and I mean really had to go so it did a very large ummm lets say numero two lol. Anyways, I was walking around it and slipped on some ice and fell right into the horse droppings. So my date said he wouldn't walk into the prom with me covered in sh*t and he ditched me for my best friend and I went into the prom alone covered in nice smelly poop!

Liz, Arts and Business, Corona, Queens NY

Well, I finally arrived at my prom, about 20 minutes late because of my dumb limo driver. My date was waiting for me at the door like a perfect gentleman. We absolutely made an entrance. For some reason everyone said I looked sssssooo sexy. But they said it in such a way I felt something was wrong and I didn't think they were serious. So my date and I sat down and wondered what everyone was looking at. He then looked at me and his face turned red and he nearly threw up right on my $425 DRESS. He ran off to the bathroom like a big baby. I started smelling something funky and then I noticed that I had sat on my dog's leftover from his meatloaf. I started crying hysterically and I soon went home. Now, whenever any of those people see me or my man they call out barf and doodlehead coming at ya!

One of a Kind

This is a cheating category. What "One of a Kind" really means is that the stories below don't fit into categories such as "The Whole Dress Goes Whoosh." These stories are so unique—and funny—that they are in no category at all. There are plenty of unexpected ways the magician's show can go wrong. The possibilities are endless, as you will see.

Junior, Shenfield High School, London ON
My date and I decide to go 2 the prom separately. When I arrived I wondered why the door was locked and no one else was there. So, thinking it woz a prank I decided to climb through an open window. It was not until I had fallen in and lay sprawled on the floor that I realized I had fallen into the middle of a wake! I had gotten the wrong venue!! It was so embarrassing and I had to apologize to the guests and try to explain why I had climbed through the window. I then tried to find the right venue and of course missed the meal and everything. Oh well, it was a laugh!!!!!

Katrina, St. Pius High School, Ottawa ON
My boyfriend picked me up for our prom dance last year. Everything was fine until we got there and two of my friends had the same dress as me. But one thing was not the same: a big booger was hanging down out of my nose. To top it all off my boyfriend was totally grossed out and would not dance with me.

Jaclyn, Nobel School, Denver CO
It all started on the day of the prom. I had a very nasty cold so I stayed home from school that day and didn't know if I could make it to prom that night. So the day goes by and I am still feeling like crap, and I decide to go to prom anyway. A little while later the phone rings and

it's my boyfriend, who is my date, and I tell him the reason I wasn't at school was that I was out getting last minute stuff and getting my hair and nails done. So I go to prom looking like a ghost and hoping no one will notice. Finally I meet up with my boyfriend and everyone is dancing, even him, and with another girl! and I ask if I can cut in, but he tells me and everyone else he doesn't know me and has never heard of me (nice boyfriend!). So I leave to go to the ladies room, and as I am in the stall I can hear two girls whispering to one another about a girl coming to prom looking like she put on white face paint (me!). So I walk out and both of them are staring and laughing at me so I ignore them. As I am walking to my so called "BOYFRIEND" everyone is looking at me and laughing and I say, "What are you staring at?" and some chick says, "Check out the toilet paper, ghost!" So I turn around and see a huge trail of toilet paper leading from the bathroom into my underwear!!!

Heather, Putnam High School, Putnam CT

It was my junior prom. It was okay. I had a great time, and one of my really good guy friends was my date. I got a dress that was periwinkle and it was so cute, it made me feel really pretty with the pearls that wrapped around my neck, and my hair all pulled up and everything. When we got to prom we sat down and talked, got our pictures taken by the roving cameraman. When I looked down at the table, I thought that the tablecloth looked really pretty. Then it hit me that the table-cloth and napkins were the same exact color as my dress. For the rest of the night I would have to stand up if I needed to find my napkin because I kept losing it on my dress. Then when the waitress came to take the plates and napkins away she asked if my napkin was part of my dress or not. When I handed it to her, I blushed and said, "No, I just planned this really well!"

Cassandra, Glens Falls High School, Glens Falls NY

My dress was amazing! It was red with a hand-beaded top with beads trailing all the way down and it had fifteen layers. I loved that dress! The only problem was that it was so large and heavy that I couldn't lift it myself to go to the bathroom. So I had to ask the chaperones if my boyfriend could help me. I never thought I would ever get a look like the one I got from a teacher—but they let me. :-)

Jessica, Kennedy TX

My school is really small, and so our prom includes freshmen and sophomores. Anyhoo, my freshman year at prom we were doing the chicken dance, and I guess I got pulled a little too hard on the hand (when our hands were joined and we were running around in a circle). Well, I fell on my stomach, and the two friends on either side of me were dragging me bumping along across the floor for like fifteen feet. I'm a total klutz, so I don't get embarrassed too much by stuff like that...it was really funny!

Alicia, St.Clair High, Robertsville MO

I was at my boyfriend's house meeting his dad for the first time when his brother noticed something with strings on the ground. When he picked them up they looked just like the new tie underwear that I had bought for the night. I was so embarrassed that I almost didn't say they were mine. But I thought about how much they had cost me, so I said oops, that it was the fact that I was wearing a very long, large dress and that I kept pulling it up, probably pushing the underwear down. Gotta love gravity!

Anonymous

My dad is waaaay overprotective but surprisingly, he did let me take a date to prom. So the guy comes and picks me up at my house and my father looks abnormally happy. I expected him to be mean, short, and evil to my date. Instead, he's totally quiet and smiling as I'm getting ready. But as we're about to walk out the door, he says, "Let's all hold hands and go to God in prayer." I thought I was going to faint! I mean, I would have understood it if my father was a preacher or even an avid churchgoer. But he goes to church maybe three times in the year, and it was obvious that he was doing it to freak out my date and totally devastate me. Then he proceeds to say a 10-minute prayer—10 whole minutes!—on the value of abstinence and a "What Would Jesus Do" thing. It was horrible. Finally, my date and I, both completely freaked out, with me sweating and everything, at last get to leave. Fortunately though, my dad didn't scare my date away for good because he asked me to prom again this year. I just have to PRAY that history doesn't repeat itself!

Joella, Spiro High School, Spiro OK

My friend wore a black and white dress with lots of feathers on it around the neck. They played the chicken dance and my friends started laughing at her. But I thought she looked more like a buzzard.

Adrian, Oak High School, CA

I was having fun with my friends when my mom shows up and says I forgot my underwear in the dryer and that she brought them to me but that they were all soggy. Everybody heard her and my date left me....

Caroline, Manasquan HS, Manasquan NJ

So, it was prom night...the most exciting night of my life! I was going with my boyfriend, who was a year ahead of me. The day before, I got a full body wax because I am a little hairy. I had gotten my mustache waxed, my legs, my arms, and my back. I guess I was allergic to the wax or something, but I had a reallllly bad reaction to it. My dress was a little skimpy so it showed a lot of my skin. When my date finally came, my mom wanted to take some pictures. I didn't want to because the reaction would be visible. I argued with my mother but I lost and she took her precious pictures, preserving my waxing on film for ever. So after that was over my date asked me, "What is wrong with your face?" So I told him that I had got it waxed. All night he couldn't leave it alone, and he kept pointing out all the rashes on my body. It was really embarrassing. And since he kept doing this in front of our friends, I had to tell people that the rash was from the body wax. So then all these people were going around announcing that I'm so hairy I had to get waxed!

Sarah, Lancaster High, Lancaster PA

It was prom night...my first one. I was a sophomore, my date was a junior. I was looking my very best to impress him, and he was obviously trying to impress me, because he looked absolutely amazing! He did, however, have braces. I also had braces. That night we got really close and he kissed me. Someone knocked into him while we were kissing and we hit foreheads, so I pulled back. There was a problem though, and when I tried to back up, I couldn't. Our braces had caught. It was sooo embarrassing. We went away from the crowd and finally got them unhooked. We didn't kiss again until he got his removed a week later.

Kaili, Miami FL

It was my senior prom. My date had stood me up and my mother had to take me to prom. I was very aggravated and almost stayed home. But I decided to go. I was kind of hungry, so we stopped at Taco Bell. I ate in the car, and jumped out when we arrived. As soon as I walked in, the yearbook committee snapped a picture of me. I wanted to know how it looked, so I took my mirror out and noticed I had a big blob of taco meat stuck between my two front teeth. Aaargghh!

Laurenne, Westside High School, Houston TX

So it was my senior prom. I was all ready to go and happy because this was my last year. All through my high school years everyone, including my boyfriend, John, laughed at me because my last name is McDonalds. Yes, just like the food chain...which I refuse to eat in. So we got to the prom and they were announcing the most outrageous people in the whole year, and suddenly they called my name. So I walked up to the stage for my prize and there she was, last year's queen with a bunch of cheeseburgers from McDonalds!!! I just wanted to kill myself....And my boyfriend John? He acted like he didn't know me and ignored me the whole night!!!!!

Anonymous, TX

It was at the after-prom party and the school had rented all these casino card tables (complete with dealers from the company) and slot
machines. Of course, everyone was hooked on the slot machines
because they are so addicting yet fun. Remember, this was play money
we were betting with so it wasn't illegal or anything. As I was leaving a
slot machine after I had given up, my little dish with my betting chips
and coins for slots fell on the floor. Well, I decided to go back to the
main area and after I picked up my stuff from the floor, I said, "OK!
Now we can go, baby!" right in front of all the senior class. I must
have had the word "baby" in my head because I call my little dog that
all the time so it must have just slipped out. Hopefully, the hott guy I
have been crushing on since the beginning of this year didn't hear me
in the next room! I was so embarrassed even if no one might have
heard me!!

Anonymous

I was a freshman and a pretty hott one at that. But anyway, I had the
star senior as my date for prom, and everything was going cool. I
had other seniors and juniors wanting my number, and so I was happy
as a little lark. There was a girl at prom that wanted the guy I was with.
He was her ex. Well when I went into the b room to do a number one
she had gone in there a minute before me and I saw her leaving just as
I went in. We passed at the door and she gave me a funny little smile.
Anyway, all the stalls were locked except one, which is the one she had
been in, so I went in and went to the bathroom and she had Saran
Wrapped the toilet! GRRRRRRR!!!!

Beat That!

Every now and then so much happens to one person on prom night that it's hard to believe this could be for real. But as they say, truth is stranger than fiction. And for the following stories, yes, I would have to agree. The only magic left here is that they survived the night at all!

Danielle, Hillcrest P.S, London ON
It was my grade eight graduation, and as a tradition all the grads walk onto the stage, say their name into the microphone, and what high school they're going to. Well I was really excited because I got to walk out just after my crush, except that I went too fast and bumped into him on the stage. I tried to back off but my heel broke and I fell. If that wasn't bad enough, when I went to stand up, my best friend came to help me, and because her dress was poorly sewn, I accidentally stepped on it and the whole bottom ripped off, leaving her standing in only her thong. And if that wasn't enough, a strap had also broken off my dress, so that it too fell down and left me standing there with my boobs showing!

That was the worst graduation ever!!

Stephanie
Prom started at 7:00, but I was going at 8:30 so that everyone could notice me arriving fashionably late. Well, I was on my period. I had a light peach dress on, and I was wearing a thong. Well, when we came in they were about to announce king and queen. Well, I was cheering for the prom queen when they said the queen is…Stephanie…I ran onto the stage and gave a 10-minute speech…until the principal stopped me and said I wasn't prom queen, that it was the other Stephanie. Horrified, I ran back off the stage, tripped and went rolling down the stairs, my dress ripped, my thong broke, everyone

saw my pad, and the next day they put *that* picture in the yearbook!!! I didn't go to school for four days!

Anonymous, Charlston High School, NY

My best friend and I went shopping a couple of months before prom, and we found two beautiful dresses. My friend wanted me to get the black one, but I bought the white one. My friend got really really really mad and stopped talking to me. Eventually, it was the night of prom. My date and I went over to the food table and were admiring the huge chocolate layer cake. Just then, my best friend (the one that was no longer talking to me) came over. I thought that she was going to apologize, but she picked up the entire cake and threw it at me. I had 10 pounds of chocolate icing down the front of me. I looked to my date for some help, but he just laughed and walked away, hand in hand, with my ex-best friend. To make it worse, my mum called the radio station and all of our relatives to tell them what happened. I was so mad at my mum and date that I went to live with my grandparents in another state. At least I know they won't make fun of me for it!!!!

Alexia, Honolua High School, Honolua HA

It was supposed to be the perfect night. I had this awesome dress and the hottest—I mean hotttt—and popular guy to go with me to the prom. So finally the night arrives and they're just about to announce prom queen when the geek of the school started singing about how much he loves me and they have police escort him off the stage. So after that embarrassing moment they finally announce prom queen and I was the winner and when I walked up on stage this person that didn't want me to win grabbed the punch bowl and hurled it at me. On top of that my date didn't win prom king and a person that I didn't like did and so we had to dance that dance together and he stepped on my dress, pulling it down right at the moment when the newspaper reporters were taking a picture of us!! AND ON TOP OF THAT we were put in the newspaper with a picture of me with my boobs out!!!!!!!!! That is it!

Hilary, CHS, MI

Alright, it was my junior prom. My girlfriend & I made a prom dinner for our boyfriends, so it could be cozy and personal. While we were eating dessert, some of it fell out of my mouth onto my dress. Well, I reached for it, picked it up and put it back in my mouth! My date was grossed out, and I couldn't believe I'd done that (too much sparkling cider I think)! So, I had a stain on my pretty dress, and you can even see it in our picture (two other people were also wearing my dress...grrr). THEN, at the dance, one of my friends told me my mom was at the entrance. I didn't believe him, but went to check anyway. Truly, she and my sister were there, and told me we had had a fire at my house! I was so upset, thinking I didn't have a house anymore, that I wouldn't even let my girlfriend hug me (to make me feel better). Well, I went home to pack, and nothing was even wrong—it just smelled a little funny inside. I felt so stupid that I had been bawling & grouchy to my date! So I went back to the dance (I made it about two minutes before it was over), and we went to after-prom activities. THERE, my girlfriend, me, and our dates sat together again. So, we were taking memory pictures and everything, & my boyfriend decided to give me a little memento—a picture of him licking my face! I don't really want to throw it away, but everyone teases me about it. After prom, I couldn't go back home yet, so I slept at my girlfriend's house. However, I slept in my makeup, so in the morning (afternoon, actually, since I slept 'til 2pm) I looked terrible—my makeup was all smeared, and my eyes were black from smudged mascara. Hopefully this year will go better!

Kiki, Gerald Ford High School, Peachville GA

OK, so, this absolutely gorgeous guy asked me to prom my senior year, and I was totally stoked! So anyway, he came and picked me up at my house, and my parents were nowhere to be found (luckily), so he goes to put on the corsage, and pokes me with the pin, but I'm anemic and started bleeding all over my dress. Luckily my older sister had a spare in her room so I put that one on! Then we were driving (in his beater car), and one of his tires goes flat!! We stood outside for like an hour waiting for someone to help us ('cause he had no idea how to change a flat, and I wasn't gonna try in my spike heels). So we had to skip dinner 'cause we missed our reservation, so we went straight to prom. As we were walking in the door, the first thing I hear from someone is, "Kiki-kins!" I was horrified to see that it was my mother, who was a chaperone. I hadn't known that my parents would be there. I thought they were at a dinner together. I was mortified! So anyway, I tried to get over that and the fact that I was wearing my sister's old dress that looks like it is straight from 1989, with stupid frills and strapless and white. We were on our way to the dance floor to get our groove on, but since we hadn't eaten dinner, my date offered to get me some snack and punch, so I told him to meet me at the table while I said hi to some friends on the dance floor. Then, to my surprise, my parents decided that they needed to dance as well! They were totally embarrassing me on the dance floor, and they were in the middle of a dance circle, getting jiggy with it, and my mom was shimmying, and my dad was trying to do the worm. I did my best to get over that, but as I turned around to see if anyone was watching my reactions, my date walked up and I knocked the punch out of his hand, all over my white, now red tie-dyed, dress. As I tried to stop the punch from getting on me, I took a step back and stepped on the back of my dress, and little did I know that someone thought it would be funny to untie the back of it (which was held on with ties all up the back), so the entire thing fell off, exposing my naked body to everyone including my parents. All I was wearing was a black thong! I ran to the bathroom as fast as possible, but on my way they announced that I was prom queen, so I had to get my dress on really fast and go up there to receive my crown. The stupid juniors bought butt-ugly crowns, and I was stuck with the queen one. Don't get me wrong, I was so excited to be queen, but the crown was just so hideous. Then they announced that the king was my ex-boyfriend, who I broke up with after last prom when I found him making out with my best friend. So we had to dance together in front of everyone with my dress practically falling off. Then my ex decided it would be funny to pull it off again, in front of everyone. Guh. Then I was so hungry that I went to snack on the appetizers and someone tripped and the entire punch bowl and snack table came tumbling down on me. Then my date was so embarrassed at my appearance that he took off with some other girl (in his beater car, so that wasn't so bad), but I ended up having to ride home with my parents!!! I was so incredibly mortified that I didn't go to school the entire next week!! So that's my horrible prom story. BEAT THAT!!

TRADITIONS

Introduction

Marriage in the US and Canada has a fairly typical core structure that makes it recognizable as marriage and not some other ceremony. Some of the elements in this core structure include the groom not seeing the bride until she is at the altar, the father giving the bride away by walking her down the aisle, the best man holding the rings, the couple exchanging vows, and so on. Within this core structure, though, there are all kinds of regional variations: in one area, or one denomination, the bride and groom read vows to each other; in another the priest or reverend reads the vows; in still another the bride wears a veil, while elsewhere she appears without one; in another, they not only exchange rings, but leis; and so on. These are all variations on a basic ceremonial structure; we call them local customs, or traditions, wherever we encounter them. It's as if there's a master script somewhere that dictates the overall shape of the marriage ceremony, but not all the details of that script are filled in. So you either fill in your own depending on where you live and what your local traditions are, or you write in a few embellishments to come up with something new (but which still fits into the overall script).

It's exactly the same for prom. There is definitely a master script out there, which means that all schools that have proms and grads have recognizably similar proms and grads. But then there are the details, and this is where the differences arise. This is where the local customs, or traditions, exist.

Now, traditions don't mean much unless they exist as traditions within a larger framework. If there is no larger framework (the master script), then you don't have a tradition; you have something totally new and outside the envelope—and we know that's not the case where prom is concerned. What is this basic larger framework within which local prom traditions exist? Here is a short outline—the master script itself. Bear in mind as you consider it that a) not all schools and prom-goers include every element I describe here, and b) all schools and prom-goers enact their own particular variations of the script.

The Master Prom Night Script

Prom night takes place at or near the end of the school year. It happens in the school gym or in a suitable hall. The place is always decorated according to a theme chosen earlier in the year. When the day of prom arrives, students either skip that whole day (if it's a Thursday or Friday) or part of it, and go home to prepare for the evening. The girls spend most of the day getting ready. They go to their hair and nail appointments. Or they primp at home with friends, do their makeup, and fuss over their dresses. Then they wait for their dates to pick them up. The guys, on the other hand, spend the day relaxing or hanging out, and only get ready at the last minute. They arrive at their dates' houses in limos or other fancy transportation. There is that initial, symbolic moment when she either descends the stairs or comes out of her room and her date sees her for the first time. They then exchange corsages and boutonnieres. The family takes pictures.

Often, prom night includes a grand march, where parents and the entire community may gather to watch the prom-going couples be formally presented. This may take place where the dance is being held, or in another officially designated and appropriately decorated locale. After the grand march, the couple leaves to dinner, or dinner is provided at the prom hall and they go there directly. Arrival at the prom hall is a second symbolic moment and the entrance is usually adorned to symbolize passage into a magical realm. Once inside, the couples sit and chat, or they dance. They pose for prom pictures. Prom court is held and the king and queen are crowned. The king and queen share a dance. Couples now start to leave. Many couples leave early.

"After-prom" begins. One of two things now happens. Couples may go to a "safe prom" sponsored by the school or parents, which is all fun and games but chaperoned and alcohol-free. Safe prom lasts all night and in the morning couples and friends go out to breakfast. Then they go home and prom night, including after-prom, is over. If they are not going to safe prom, couples instead rent hotel rooms to party in with groups of friends, or they attend a party somewhere. These parties also go all night (and sometimes people leave "safe prom" to attend one of these). In the morning, party-goers sleep or go to breakfast. At some point in the day everyone goes home and prom night is over.

Sometimes, prom night continues on into an after-prom that lasts the weekend. Couples and friends go camping. Or they rent cottages on lakes. Or they go to theme parks. The after-prom weekend is more typical of senior than junior prom.

This is the master prom script as it is enacted each year in schools all over North America. Every school, and I mean every school that has prom, enacts a version of that script: that's why prom is recognizable as prom no matter where it happens. The local differences as each school enacts the script, however, are often radical—because no two schools enact the master script in exactly the same way. Some schools stick fairly close to the script and introduce only minor variations. But some schools have developed traditions over the years that really change or add to the master script (without distorting it out of recognition). Below, I have included a sampling of these traditions (with commentary), ranging from those that stick to the script to those with really exotic variations. As you read these local traditions, ask yourself, "How much does this tradition deviate from the master script?" You may be amazed to find that not only does it not deviate at all (in the sense that it ruins or replaces the master script), but that somehow it perfects the master script by making that local prom night perfect for its prom-goers. And that's the most interesting thing about traditions in general: they are not there to break away from the master script, but to complement and bring it that much more fully into life. In other words, traditions are what personalize the general script and give it its local flavor (its individual emotional content). But read on, read on!

Traditional Prom Night
and Proto-Prom

In these first two stories, prom night sticks fairly close to the master
script and you can see all the basic elements at play. It's not that these
two schools don't have unique traditions. Rather, theirs are traditional
proms.

Sarah, Frisco TX

Our prom traditions are the same as anyone else's, I suppose, except
for a few alterations to the night in question. Prom is always on a
Saturday night. This year it's going to be held at Southfork Ranch
(where they taped the TV show "Dallas"). We always have the girls at
one house getting ready, the guys at another, and then when everyone
is ready we all go to a third person's house to take pictures (usually the
one with the best looking banister/staircase). After pics we head to
some fancy restaurant in Dallas, then after eating we head to prom.
Nobody ever stays for the whole prom....After dancing, checking out
everyone else's dresses, taking even more pics, and talking to a few
administrators, everybody heads out to IHOP/Denny's, and then to
PARTIES!! We may be from the South, but we do know how to party!
Hotels usually "forget" to check the IDs of partygoers checking in (you
are supposed to be 25). All in all it's a hell of a lot of fun and everybody gets completely smashed and doesn't go home until Sunday
evening if at all!! We are the coons, the mighty mighty coons!

Jade, IL

My prom is usually held in April or May. It's always on a Saturday
night from 6-11. That Saturday, girls spend all sorts of time getting
ready and making themselves beautiful for their dates. At about 3:00
the guys start picking their dates up (oh yeah, it's jr/sr unless you're

asked by one of those). Pictures are taken and then it's off to the school gym for Promenade. The gym is decorated with some sort of red carpet down the middle and chairs on either side. This is when dates get shown off and more pictures are taken. You wait in line for an hour to get your name called and then you walk down the red carpet with your date. After that everyone loads up into limos, buggies, cars, etc. and goes to the nearby town for dinner and the dance. The dinner is never very good, but there's entertainment by the master and mistress of ceremonies (usually 2 seniors) until the dance starts. At 8 the DJ starts playing songs and everyone heads to the dance floor. Most people only stay a couple hours (while dancing is going on a pro photographer is taking pictures). After prom the school hosts post-prom, which has always been at the school in past years, but this year is being held at this university recreational building. If you choose to go there, there's always food, games, karioke, etc. But most of the seniors opt to get a hotel room together (usually more than one) and all the seniors have one final party before graduation, which isn't very far away!

Prom night in Canada is only for seniors. Prom night in the US is always for seniors, but there may also be one for juniors, depending on the size of the school. Rarely, there is one for ninth graders. The story below is a ninth grade prom. Note as you read that most of the master script is already there. That's what makes it prom, and not Winter Ball or Sadie Hawkins, or some other dance.

Kyla, Puyallup WA

My first prom is this year! All of the junior highs throw the first prom for the 9th graders. They do it in June and each school is in charge of something different. The prom is held at a big hall at the local fairgrounds (kinda weird place, I know) and before it, everyone goes out for dinner. Most of those who have dates are only going with them as friends, and it's mostly groups of people that go together. Then after the prom the whole group of whomever you go with goes to someone's house and just hangs out there. Sometimes it's just 'til like 2 or 3 a.m. and sometimes it's the whole night! The next day you get up and everyone wears their dresses/tuxes to school. That day's also usually the last day of school and all the 7th & 8th graders get to see how everyone looked.

Canadian Prom Night

Proms are a little different in Canada than they are in the US. In the US proms can be, but do not have to be, linked to graduation. They are not often either preceded or followed by a cap and gown ceremony. In Canada on the other hand, there is usually only one prom (which is also called grad), and it happens senior year. So yes, it's linked with graduation and the whole cap and gown scene. Here's a Canadian tradition that exemplifies this model, but includes a pretty cool moment with the teachers. It not only shows how the graduating seniors are becoming the symbolic "equals" of their teachers, but also places the location for this equality in a college setting to emphasize the importance of the grad transition.

Jolie, Kamloops BC

At my school it's traditional to have the prom at the local college. The night before the actual prom is a Friday night—a school night. However, all of the grads sit down to a fancy catered dinner with the teachers (at the college centre). The grads then proceed to the gym to have the actual ceremony (with gowns and hats and commencement). It's kind of a neat tradition. The next night, Saturday, is the prom. The grads and their parents participate in what we call the "grand march," which is where they are all dressed up and march around the college activity centre, showing off their dresses and tuxes. (It's kinda like a wedding ceremony, now that I think about it.) After the march the grads have their prom, which is the big dance, followed by all the parties afterward.

The following Canadian prom/grad is closer to the master script than the last story because it's just the graduation ceremony followed by the prom party and the after-party. What I'd like to draw your attention to is the alcohol issue. These prom-goers have a "safe prom" that doesn't mean, "Don't drink," but, "Drink in a safe environment," with parents and teachers present. The drinking age being lower in Canada than in the US, this isn't particularly problematic for Canadians.

Tasha, Beaverlodge AB

I come from a small town whose high school includes kids from all the other surrounding towns. We kind of have grad and prom together. Every year it's held on the first Friday of June and at 3:00 the whole class meets at the research station to get pictures. From there everyone does whatever until 6:30, when we go to the arena for grad. At the arena, each person walks up on the stage for their "diploma." As they receive the diploma, someone reads a little rhyming poem their friends have written about them. The poems are usually so hilarious everyone's busting a gut. Then after the ceremonies everyone goes to the curling rink for the first couple of dances. From there, everyone changes into jeans and hoodies and takes their liquor to the sports grounds to be taken to the party. Everyone then gets a bracelet and gets on the school's buses to take us all to the "safe grad," which is a big huge bonfire with everyone drinkin' lots and havin' a great time. We kick ass!!!!!

Here's another Canadian prom/grad tradition. This one is a nice variation on the basic theme. Parents get involved, the graduation ceremony is held, the dance comes, and then the rest of the weekend is a long party that integrates prom night into larger, town-wide, even Canada-wide celebrations.

Anonymous, BC

Well I live in a really small town of about 2500 people so my senior class only has around 65 or so kids. But we have lots of fun on prom night. Every year, graduation ceremonies and prom are held on June 30th/July1st. Our town has something that we call "Wildcat Days," which is a big celebration that coincides with grad weekend and Canada Day. So the big day starts when you wake up the morning of the 30th. Usually everyone skips school the day before and goes for a hike or a camp out in the mountains that surround our town. Then, when you wake up on the 30th, you rush home from camping and get dressed in your robe and cap and head to the school. They have decorations based on the theme that the grad class gets to choose. We walk through the crowd in a pattern, in time with grad music (we've rehearsed this earlier in the year). After that we all end up on the stage in alphabetical order and have our names called out to get our diplomas. Then the three people who were chosen to be class historians read the speech they prepared about everything that we've all been through since grade 8 together. The class valedictorian (who is elected by the students) also reads his/her speech (basically, the valedictorian is chosen in grade 8 and everyone knows who it'll be from that time on). After that there is a meet and greet people session in the gym where everyone can socialize with everyone else and everybody's families from everywhere are there. That usually happens around 12:30-1:00 in the afternoon. Once all that is over, we go prepare for the dance. Since there are only two hair salons in our town, the girls have to schedule their appointments about 6 months in advance, and the girls who don't do it quick enough will have to go to towns a half hour away. So all that starts, and then it's home to get dressed and take pictures. Usually it's customary for you and your date (also basically picked in grade 8) to have a few drinks with your parents...then a designated driver or parents will drive you to meet friends. Then group pics are taken and people do whatever until 8 when prom starts. At this time everyone packs into the gym and the grad class does another choreographed grand march. This dance is usually very complicated but it's really cool when it's done right...it's in the dark with lasers and crazy lights flashing in exact time with the grand march song (which is also picked by the grad class). After that there is the father/daughter, mother/son dance. And then people can just hang out as long as they

want. Right before midnight everyone at prom (EVERYONE!) goes to
the ballpark to watch the Canada Day fireworks which go off at 12.
Once that's over everyone gets to go change their clothes and get stuff
packed up to go to dry grad party. Now, this is held at the swimming
pool and arena complex. It has everything, door prizes (trips to
Hawaii, Mexico, CD players, cell phones, computers, everything!).
It's tradition to see who can stay on the mechanical bull the longest.
And the swimming pool is open all night too (usually along with her
prom dress, each girl buys a new really expensive bathing suit to wear
to dry grad). The next morning everyone goes home and sleeps for a
few hours and then attends all the Canada Day/Wildcat Day activities.
It's definitely a great year and I'm looking forward to it a lot!!!

One more tradition out of Canada. This one takes place in the
province of Quebec. If you've been there, then you know that in many
ways, Quebec isn't like the rest of Canada. It's mostly French speaking, although there's a strong English mix, mostly in Western Quebec
and in the city of Montreal. On this occasion, however, the different
language and culture does not appear to affect the master prom script,
which remains intact. As usual, there are the expected local traditional
variations; but there's nothing so different about Kelly's prom night,
below, that it tempts you to say, "Hey, wait a minute, that's not prom."
So here's how they do it in bilingual Montreal.

Kelly, Montreal QC

Prom in Montreal is called grad. It is amazing! On Friday morning,
all the girls get their hair, nails, make-up done. Then we go home
and get picked up by the limo. At 6 we go to school for a (non-alco-
holic) cocktail with the teachers and to take our group picture. Then
we have an hour to drive around. We usually go to the lookout, which
is on the mountain in the middle of the city and overlooks all of
Montreal, and we take more pictures. Then we go to the hotel. Our
parents are invited to the dinner and dance, which lasts 'til about 12.
Then we all get changed and go clubbing (usually the Dome) 'til 2 or

3. Then we go party hopping. One person has a big party for the whole grade—with kegs!—and others rent hotel rooms. At 6am we all go to breakfast, where everyone looks very hungover and very tired (most usually wear sunglasses). Then we go home to crash for a few hours. Saturday afternoon we go camping at someone's country house (we went up to Standstead). That night we get totally trashed. Then Sunday we drive back and someone has a pool party. We usually get home Sunday night at 9:00pm. Our grad is 3 days long. Though it's really expensive, there's nothing like it.

United States: Small Towns

Back to the US now. As far as concerns our master script idea, in the US we can divide proms into those that are held in small towns and those held in the large ones, or cities. While the basic script remains the same, the traditions between town and country are bound to differ. One thing you notice right at the outset about small towns is the increased participation of parents, and even the entire community. Because they can, the whole town may turn out to watch the prom-goers promenade in their finery before the dance begins. What stands out about the local prom tradition is what they do for that one special couple....

Krista, Soldotna AK

Prom at Soldotna High School is always very elegant. In a small town like mine people make a huge deal out of it. We have our promenade before the dance so the community can come in and see how everyone is dolled up in their gowns and tuxedos. Every year there is one couple (a different couple each year) that trades roles as the boy and girl. It is absolutely hilarious to see a boy (usually a jock) dressed in an evening gown and pumps and to see a girl in a tuxedo. Even though they do this, our prom is still classy, and those who attend are well mannered and refined...for one night anyway!

In this next small town prom night, parents and community also turn out to see their prom-goers. However, it introduces a variant into the master prom script that has caught on over the past twenty years or so, the grand march. Grand marches are more typical of small towns than large ones (mostly for logistical reasons). In essence, they re-enact the original Victorian upper class "promenade," the actual moment of walking into the hall or room along with a formal presentation of the individual or couple. During the grand march, the dressed-up couples are formally presented for the first time to the waiting community. The interesting local variant here, is that the guy puts the garter on his date during the grand march. Elsewhere, the garter event either happens informally during the dance as the guys and girls play around, or more formally but still during the dance, where it is orchestrated by the master of ceremonies. Another variant that stands out in the story below is the prom dinner held before the dance. The mothers of the juniors prepare it, and the sophomores serve it. I draw your attention to this because it shows how, in smaller towns, a larger portion of the community may participate directly—as more than bystanders—in the celebration.

Jamie, Sargent School, Monte Vista CO

The Sargent School prom is a junior/senior prom. It's held in our gym and the junior class has to put it together. Before the dance we have dinner in our cafeteria. The mothers of the juniors make the dinner and the food has to do with the prom theme (oh yeah, you have a different dress for dinner). Sophomores from our school are the ones that serve the dinner and they are dressed up like something that has to do with our theme. After dinner you go back to your house and change into your second dress. You then go back to school and have your pictures taken and then wait around until 9pm for the grand march. That is where your parents and anyone from the community can come and see how everyone looks. You enter with your date and then the guy will put the garter on your leg and then you leave and watch everyone from the side. The dance lasts 'til about midnight and then you head off to after-prom. That's held at the bowling alley or some place like that. You eat, hang out, play poker, and that all ends around 4am.

In another small town, next, the community is again central. Something to note is that in these smaller towns, roles are often assigned to community members. In this story, it's the junior students' fathers who park the prom-goers' cars. In the story you just read, it's the juniors' mothers who cook dinner for the prom-goers. These traditions are wonderful enhancements to the master prom night script because they get everyone involved, and thus it is not the prom-goers alone who look forward to prom night, but the whole community.

Grundy Center HS, Grundy Center IA

We always have prom on a Saturday night. The girls spend the whole day getting ready and about 1:00 you go for pics and that usually takes 'til about 5:30. But once you are done taking pictures you go cruising down Main. The entire community is standing on the streets watching the different cars go by and everyone in their dresses. At about 6:00 we go to the community building. The community usually gets there before us. So we each drive up in our cars and one by one we are announced as we get out of the cars. Meanwhile, the junior students' dads go and park the cars. We have dinner at the community building and then go to a club for the dance, which lasts 'til midnight. Then it's after-prom, with a hypnotist and all those fun games ;-). Then it's party time and going out for breakfast.

Small town in Kentucky this time. This prom night is very close to what I would consider the quintessential prom, one that sticks really close to the master script. But there are several local touches that make it very special indeed. Pay particular attention to what some of the guys wear to prom, and remember, this is Kentucky—theirs is the perfect local touch!

Tara, Wayne County High School, Monticello KY

I live in a small town, and go to a small high school. There aren't any malls or limo services or nice restaurants here. Our prom is combined, junior and senior. We rent the Rural Development Center in the neighboring town because it's big, nice, and has a ballroom. Most people borrow the nicest car they can get for them and their date, and prom is only from about 6:00 to 11:00. It's always on a Saturday, and the Friday before, it is Senior Layout Day...where EVERY senior lays out and we go to the lake. Since prom ends so early, the after-prom plans are usually a REALLY big deal. There are generally three choices: rent a hotel room, go to one of the major parties, or go home. There's always a rivalry to see who has the biggest party...because it's a small, small place and we generally are all friends anyhow. A lot of us wear the traditional tux and gown, but some of the guys around here wear black pants, button up white shirts, black cowboy boots, and black cowboy hats. For the most part, no one goes home prom night. We usually come home the next afternoon, and that's pretty well accepted by the parents around here.

A small town. Again, you can see the community and its traditions at work. You can also see that this is the quintessential prom, really close to the master script. What stands out in this story is how the school administration imposes a class attendance rule on those who are going to prom. The rule, however, is a formality, because while the students may be stuck in class until 11am, they certainly are not there in spirit.

Amanda, Oakfield NY

At Oakfield High School, our junior-senior prom is a big deal. It's always on a Friday night, which sucks because if you plan on attending the prom you MUST attend school until 11:00am. That is when the school says you have put in enough school for it to count as a full day. They only do this because they know that if they don't, everyone who is going to the prom will skip school on prom day. I know—stupid, but you just deal with it. It's not THAT bad. The whole senior and junior classes (at least all the girls) get out of school at 11:00—it's cool. Then, for the gals it's off to get your hair, nails and makeup done. Then, to put on your dress and do the once-over check to make sure you have everything—boutonniere, purse, camera, ticket (although it's not very important—they don't collect tickets!), and, well, your date! It's up to the different couples and groups whether they will meet at the park or whether they will meet beforehand at someone's house and go to the park in the limo together. Most of the time the girls meet at one girl's house to get picked up and the guys at a guy's house to get picked up. Then, it's off to the park. In the middle of our town we have this park called the Triangle Park because it's in the shape of a triangle formed by three streets. There is a gazebo there and it's tradition to get pictures taken at the gazebo. Everyone gets together so you can ooh and aah over their dresses and how they glammed up for the evening. Anyone from the community can come—that is, if they can find a parking spot within a half-mile from the park. Yes, it's THAT packed. Well, with over a dozen limos parked along the street, you have to park a bit down the roads. We get to the park about 5pm to meet and take pictures and then it's off to the prom (8pm-12am). Every year it's held in a different spot. Last year it was held at a gorgeous Italian Garden about an hour away. A lot of people went to Niagara Falls afterwards. This year it's going to be held at a very posh Valley Hotel/Inn. And, seeing how it's an inn, if you or your date are over 21, you rent a room and have some fun (partying of course :)! All in all, it's awesome and you just don't miss it.

Here is one final prom night tradition in a small town. Like the others, it highlights the community's importance by allowing it to participate. In this prom, it's not just the townsfolk from Port Jefferson, New York, that come to see the prom-goers; the neighboring towns come as well. Moreover, the link between prom and graduation is very explicit in this story: the latter is consciously and deliberately used as justification for the former.

Caroline, Port Jefferson NY

I go to a really small public school, about 70 kids per grade, and the senior prom is the one thing you look forward to. We also have a junior prom, which is held at a nearby catering hall. But the senior prom is amazing. It is held in our gym. All the seniors' parents work on the decorations from the beginning of the year. They think of a new theme every year, and the seniors don't know what it is until they get to the prom. There are so many people there when you pull in! Everyone from our town, and neighboring towns, come to watch the seniors walk in. People come in so many different types of cars, too. Some come in fire trucks, limos, horse and buggies, and I have even heard of someone landing in front of the school in a helicopter (which they got in trouble for). But the cool thing is that it is after graduation. We graduate on a Friday, and the prom is the following Monday. So you can really do whatever you want. And the parents are chaperones, so they really don't care what you do. And after the prom, people hang out for days, usually out on a beach somewhere. It really is a great way to end your high school life. I can't wait to go!

United States: Large Towns

So now I have shown you a few traditions from small towns, and I have said how they involve the entire community. The next one is a tradition from a large town, one of the largest in fact, Los Angeles, California. It isn't just that prom night in Los Angeles (or other large cities) cannot include the entire community. It's the very scale on which prom night takes place. Because these cities have more to offer in terms of exotic entertainment, their prom nights tend to be that much more spectacular in terms of light and location, sound and sensation. You may recall from reading some of the stories earlier in the book that at least two other proms happening in Los Angeles were held on the boat used to film the movie *Titanic*, while one prom in Dallas was held where the show "Dallas" was taped.

Does this mean proms in big cities are better than those in small towns? Definitely not. One of the most (if not the most) important things about prom is the togetherness that it inspires. There is togetherness at the individual level since you attend as couples. There is togetherness at the friendship level since you attend with all your friends. There is togetherness at the scholastic level since you attend with your entire class and most teachers. Finally, in the small towns, there is the togetherness of the larger community in which you participate—and this is one level of togetherness that is pretty much absent from prom night in the big cities. So, while you may get to have your prom at Universal Studios, as in the story below, you may not get to be seen and fussed over by your family and friends' family, or neighbors, or most of the townsfolk, many of whom you would have known since childhood. Is this an even trade-off? That's for you to decide.

Joanna, Narbonne High School, Los Angeles CA

My school's prom next year is going to be so tight! We're having it at Universal Studios in Hollywood!! The room is going to have screens where we can flash movies and things like a star background on them so that it looks like we're outside. I heard we're also going to have lasers flashing all around too. The prom is indoors as well as outdoors. The outdoors part is called "Little Paris." It's like a little street that looks like Paris or something like that. And after-prom is gonna be at Universal City Walk. But of course we have to hit up all the after prom parties!

Jess, telling us about her school's traditions below, keeps reminding us that she lives in Las Vegas. Yes, they do have a range of activities available to them in Vegas which are not available elsewhere in the US. Yes, it is a large town.

Jess, DHS, Las Vegas NV

Prom is ALWAYS held on a Saturday night, usually at some fancy place like a hotel. For the past couple of years it's been held at a beautiful country club decked out in white twinkle lights and gorgeously decorated by our student council. Prom begins with girls waking up frantically realizing they only have a few hours to get ready. They get their hair, nails, and make-up done just right and then come home or go to a friend's house to put on their dress. Their dates arrive in a stretch Navigator or Hummer limo (it's Vegas!) and they head to the mall to take pics. Afterwards they go to a really fancy restaurant like the one at the top of the Stratosphere (tallest building in Vegas, kinda like the Seattle Space Needle—beautiful view) or in the Eiffel Tower replica. After dinner they head to the country club to take more pics and dance the night away. After that, couples either head to after-parties and get drunk, or see shows like the Blue Man Group or Cirque du Soleil (lemme remind you it's Vegas). Overall, prom is one expensive night, but an event to remember!

In this next story, the city is Santa Monica. Santa Monica is just north of L.A. and has a high population density; it would be impossible for the whole town to turn out to watch the prom-goers. Instead, the parents of individual prom-goers have "champagne parties." Each household with a girl attending prom has its own. When the girl's date arrives, he enters and joins the parents in a drink. They take pictures. Then the limo carrying all the couples going in a group moves on to the next house, where the scene is repeated.

Jennifer, Santa Monica Catholic High, Santa Monica CA

On the West Coast it's a little different. Our prom at Santa Monica Catholic High is always on a Saturday, because our school knows we girls have alot of primping to do. The prom is a junior/senior event but it is presented as a gift to the seniors from the juniors. At 11am most girls at my school go to a spa to get a massage. Between 12 and 3pm you get your nails and hair done. You also go to a cosmetics counter at the mall to get your make-up done by a professional. At 4pm we charge our cell phones so parents can keep in touch with us (bummer). We then put on our dresses and when we're all dressed and ready, we go to our champagne party—a small get together we have with our families where the adults drink champagne and the children or kids under 18 drink apple cider. During that, your date arrives in the limo. He has something to drink, and you get bombarded with pictures. Then you leave to pick up the next girl (the limo already contains all the guys). Prom usually starts at 6:30pm and dinner is served at 7pm. It's always at a hotel. Coronation of the prom court is at 10:30pm, then the last dance is at midnight. After that people go clubbing at the all-ages clubs we have out here. Then all the girls end up sleeping over at one girl's house and the next morning we go to Six Flags. It's really a blast!

As above, so below. This one takes place somewhere in Westchester county, the county directly north of New York City and, as you can imagine, very crowded. Again, there is no participating greater community. Instead, the parents of the group sharing the limo get together at someone's house and have cocktails. Then the group of prom-goers piles into the limo and heads out to do its own thing.

Kristin, Westchester NY

Our prom is the last Friday of school. No seniors come to school that day; most of us spend the day getting hair done, nails, make-up, and spa treatments. Everyone in your party gets together at about 5pm for cocktails with all the parents at someone's house and then the limo will pick everyone up there, and bring us to our local hangout, the diner, for the pre-party. Then the limo will drive us all down to the city, where the actual dance is. We'll party down there, and when the prom is over, most people will stay in Manhattan for the night.

With larger towns comes the problem of larger schools and larger attendance at prom. If you have two proms, junior and senior, each with 1500 students, it's doubtful that the community will participate very much. However, at Canton High School, below, which does have 3,000 students attending its junior and senior proms, one part of the community offers an alternative to the crowded, regular prom. The alternative sounds expensive, and there doesn't appear to be any of that crazy partying you hear about afterwards, but it's definitely a Night to Remember because it preserves the fairytale magic of prom night, right down to the romantic agrarian setting.

Anonymous, Canton High School, Canton MI

Well, my school is different from most high schools. We have three high schools on one piece of property, and you have classes in all three schools. All in all, there are about 6,000 students there. We have two separate proms every year, junior prom and senior prom. But as you can imagine, with almost 1,500 juniors and 1,500 seniors, prom is really packed. We don't hold prom at our school, we go elsewhere. But because it's so crowded, I opt not to go to it, but rather to a prom alternative, offered by my church. It is called "A Night to Remember," and is held at the Grand Hotel on Mackinac Island. If you've never been there you are missing out! The hotel is beautiful and really ritzy. A room there costs $400 a night...probably more now. And you aren't allowed in the hotel after 6 unless you are dressed up. So, NTR (Night to Remember) is held Memorial Day weekend every year. On the Sunday before, we drive up to Mackinac City and stay at a hotel on the mainland. Then Monday afternoon we take the ferry over to the island. You start getting ready, which usually includes running between the hotel rooms trying to find someone that has what you need, or if someone can help you fix your hair and whatnot (already I have been asked to do 5 people's hair that night!). Then once you're all dolled up, you go down and take pictures, and you can stand on their elegant stairs and veranda to take the pictures. Then you go to dinner (a very nice dinner), and after dinner some sort of entertainment is provided. After that, you are free to roam the island, but only until 11, since Cinderella's curfew is pushed back an hour. Then the next day (we all miss school), you are free to roam the island some more, and then when you're ready to head home, you catch another ferry back to the mainland. It's pretty expensive—the ticket costs about four times what a ticket to my school's prom would cost—but you don't have to worry about transportation fees, because you're already at the hotel, and there aren't any cars allowed on the island. It's an awesome experience, and I can't wait for May to be here!

Boarding schools have prom night, too. And it seems they party as hard and happily as any other school. In this story, we get a peek into the kind of night at least one boarding school sets up—of course, it helps that the school is located near New York City.

Amanda, Kent CT

Well, I go to a boarding school in the middle of nowhere, aargh, so everyone is basically on their own for the senior prom, which is the only prom our school has. This year, it was held in May. I was a sophomore and went with my senior boyfriend of one and a half years. I remember how I was wondering, in the fall, if we would last until spring, and now there we were, beginning to plan for the most anticipated weekend of high school. I got a white, strapless gown over break, something I had always wanted, and Chris, my boyfriend, finally decided to buy a tux. Since our school doesn't get to party too much together off campus, the after-party in NYC was what everyone was looking forward to.

Anyways, the day came at last. My friend (who had actually gotten the same dress as me, although in blue) and I prepared two hours before, knowing we'd just end up waiting around (which we did anyway) if we started any earlier. Finally my boyfriend arrived at my dorm, and we headed off to the coach buses that would bring us to the country club that was hosting the prom. To get to the coach bus, we had to walk across the lawn separating the dorms from the main buildings. Walking across it, with people hanging out their windows watching, was like walking in a dream. Cameras flashed and the campus transformed into an Oscars night. My boyfriend and I, the traditional long-term couple (one of only two couples, actually) dressed in our formal attire, felt like we were on center stage, if only for the one night.

The prom itself was a blast. The old-fashioned ballroom was great for dancing, and the food was excellent. Our friends were all around, and it seemed we were all having the time. Guys got rid of their jackets and some stripped down to bowties (and pants, no shirts). The girls threw off their shoes, and we all boogied until 10pm, when everyone got real eager to get back to the dorms and change into "city" clothes.

Back on campus, we agreed to meet in a bit at our limo, and ran to our rooms to change. What a night! I grabbed my overnight bag and joined the steady crowd filtering down to meet their cars. It is a tradition at Kent to head to the city for after-prom, but this year would be especially good because a senior girl had rented out a club for only us—open bar, dancing, the works. As about 30 others squished into a super long limo, my boyfriend and I and two other couples enjoyed our private, deluxe limo and relaxed.

However, when we got to the hotel, there was a complication. The "suite" we had rented for the six of us was only two rooms, which meant that one couple would have to leave. My boyfriend, who lives in the city, was the kind one and decided we could stay at his place, where his dad would be (sigh). I got pissed. I would rather have found another bed in the hotel, just to be with everyone, and not somewhere else—it didn't matter much if I got a good night's sleep, as long as we could all keep partying together.

Anyhow, the sleeping arrangements settled, the six of us joined everyone at the club. It was crazy there. Everyone drank, even those who I'd never seen drink or party before. There were high cages to dance in and leather couches. The music was intense and we all danced 'til nearly two in the morning, when there was a cop scare and people had to be let out in groups. My boyfriend and I found our way back to his place, a few blocks away, and I crashed on the couch, totally beat. What a night!

Origins of Tradition

There's nothing more difficult than tracking down the origin of a tradition, especially one that affects the entire master script. That's because by definition, traditions have been around for a while, which means that something that happens for the first time is, obviously, not traditional. Thinking back, we can often say that this or that is a "new" tradition, and by that we mean that it has been around for less time than other traditions. For example, the garter dance—when your date removes your garter in front of everyone—is a recent prom tradition, not quite ten years old, and we know that in this case it was borrowed from the same practice in American wedding receptions. Compared to the garter dance, grand marches, which have been around for about twenty years, are older, while holding prom court, with the election of a king and queen, is older still—perhaps forty years old.

When we speak of the origin of traditions that affect the master script, then, we always mean, their origin in relation to each other—and this is a question of time. But how about the question of space? Where (not when) does a tradition originate, and how does it grow from there, spreading outward like ripples in a pond, evolving from something that happens in one place to something that happens in every place?

I wish I could answer this; but the problem is very complex because it has to do with cultural mechanics, the demonstration of which require a longitudinal study—something conducted over years—and I do not have those resources at my disposal!

We can, however, try a thought experiment—a model—and see how that explains the incorporation of a tradition into a master script. Consider this anonymously submitted story:

We have junior-senior proms because we are a very small town. It's a tradition for the junior class to decorate and set up everything for the prom. Every year, the juniors try and outdo the juniors from the previous year, and every year, the prom becomes even more beautiful. My junior class started a tradition last year: instead of just having a senior prom king and queen, we decided to have a duke and duchess for the juniors. I'm more than sure that will continue for years to come!

(Anonymous, Hondo TX)

Their senior prom includes a king and queen. This year, they also had a duke and duchess for the juniors. It is the first time they do this. OK, now imagine the following: dukes and duchesses are part of the old European royalty structure that includes kings, barons, knights, etc. Because they fit in this structure, they make sense to us and we are not surprised that dukes and duchesses may be included in prom court (in fact, it's already happening in other schools). Now, you come along and read this. You are part of a prom committee. You suggest to your committee that your school do the same. Several other schools copy you over the next few years; more schools copy them. And ten years from now, there is a new element in the master prom night script: all schools that have junior-senior proms with kings and queens, include dukes and duchesses for the juniors. And so a tradition has been born (you can end the thought experiment now).

It's always nice when the past meets the present and you hear about something happening at the place you once went to school. When you read the story below, keep in mind that before it appeared in this book, it was submitted to www.ThePromSite.Com, and that the writer is commenting on a tradition she read on the website.

Kris, Stow OH

I just read Shana's submission from Stow. I don't live there now, but I graduated and had prom in 1985. I remember that we had our prom at the Civic Theater and had the first Grand March that I had ever heard of—we used the staircase there. Of course, I was at the "old" high school, so we didn't have a nice auditorium. After prom we went bowling 'til about 3 or 4am, then some of the mothers had a breakfast at the high school from like 6am till 8am (I overslept...oops) then we went off to Cedar Point Amusement Park for Senior Day. I had a very bad sunburn for the whole day because Mr. Hanna's biology field trip ("read" have fun and skip school day) was on prom day, and I lay out in the sun too long. Right now I am hosting an exchange student from Japan and she is going to prom. They don't have such a thing in Japan so she is really excited, and enjoys reading all of your traditions very much. Have fun!

Concerning the birth of local traditions, the tradition you just read tells us that in 1985, Kris's prom year, they had the first grand march "she ever heard of." That grand march took place at about the time that grand marches were becoming integrated into the master prom script, and now the tradition at Stow, Ohio, is going strong. Here is Shana's submission, to which Kris was replying above. Shana believes it's been a tradition for a very long time at her school. In reality, it was only fifteen years old when Shana went to prom.

Shana, Stow OH

Every year on prom day, we have this thing called Grand March where all the seniors and their dates gather into the auditorium and wait at the top of the stairs. Then an announcer will announce the couples as they walk down the stairs to the center of the auditorium stage. Friends and family who came to watch take pictures and clap while the couple leaves the stage. This has been a tradition for a very long time at our school. It's always so nice to see everyone walk down the stairs all dressed up.

Most traditions resemble each other between place and place, which is fine because there's always going to be some overlap—and this overlap is what the master script is all about. Now and then, however, you get a tradition that is totally outside what is normal for prom. Usually, when it is too far outside, it does not incorporate into the script. To incorporate it would require changing too many elements of the script, and the final result might change the very nature of the script—instead of prom, it would become something else.

I am not saying that the tradition you are about to read is not prom. But I am saying it is not part of anything we understand as contemporary prom. This tradition—a tradition only in retrospect—has been around at Aquin Catholic High since the early 1930s, when it was first created. It has not changed since. So perhaps, instead of looking at a tradition, we may actually be looking at a little piece of what prom used to be like, before it evolved into its contemporary form.

Ashley, Freeport IL

I attend Aquin Catholic High School, where our prom is quite the unique situation. We don't have the stress of whether or not you'll get asked, because we draw for our dates. Our school is small and all the students are friends so no one minds who goes with who. Choosing dates is the best part. The girls cover themselves in sheets and brown paper bags. And they wait. The guys draw from a bin in another room and then they must find their date under the sheets and bags. The guys also dress up and prepare funny skits as they ask the girl to prom, and in the past they have done everything from UPS delivery guy, to convicts that need to be set free, to Romeo quoting to Juliet on the balcony, to The Blues Brothers, The Village People, and even Adam Sandler serenading his date. The tradition is not mandatory and every year the students vote whether or not to have the draw. It's always yes! And the tradition has been going on since the early 1930s, when the school began. The NBC "Today" show has even documented our Prom Draw ceremonies. It is definitely a memorable experience!

Snippets of Tradition

This next batch of eleven story snippets contains some unique local traditions. When you read these, remember that for every tradition told here, there are hundreds, perhaps thousands that are not being told. Remember, too, that every school and town has prom in its own way, and the master script is just the point of departure for some wonderful local customs. In fact, to put all this differently, we could actually say that there is no such thing as a quintessential prom, a prom that is the exact embodiment of the master script. Every school and town has a prom that is unique to them—they do not first access a master script in order to stage their prom. Unlike a theatrical presentation or a movie, where you start with a master script and move on from there, in the case of prom night the master script only appears once you've compared hundreds of individual proms from all over North America. Collecting, comparing, and extracting what is similar to all of them—that is what generates the master script.

Corrina, Burns High School OR
Sounds kinda freaky...but every year right before prom is over...all the guys get out on the floor and take the girls' garters off with their teeth! It's quite an interesting sight...we also have junior jesters in addition to king and queen.

Jema, ID
Well our proms here are pretty different. Flowers are a huge part of the celebration. Yes, the guys do the traditional corsage buying, but couples go to the florist together to ensure matching flowers, and we not only wear corsages but almost everybody wears flowers in their hair. Last year I wore a chaplet (head wreath) made of tiny roses and my fav flower, hydrangea. This year some of my friends have plans to

attach a trailing cluster of flowers to the back of their dresses. It's kind of Victorian looking, and gorgeous!

JoJo, Scottsdale AZ

One thing that our school does is have a video contest to get people excited for Prom. It's for the most clever way to ask your date to prom. And you do it on video. The best one gets a free ticket!!

Anonymous, Kona HI

In Hawaii, the guy gives the girl a bouquet, as usual, but the girl gives the guy a lei made of a vine called a maile. It's very traditional and can be anywhere from one strand to about seven strands thick. It symbolizes many things, including love or friendship. I think that it looks really classy, and because the maile has no flowers, it looks very masculine and goes well with a tux!

Anonymous, Chesapeake VA

A big tradition for us is that every year the day before prom all the seniors skip that day and hang out at the beach and just have fun. Another big tradition is that only seniors are allowed to wear white dresses to prom. No underclassmen are allowed to wear white. And only seniors can wear white tuxedos. It's seniors' last night together and that's what distinguishes us from the underclassmen that are at our prom. And finally the day after, we all go to either Busch Gardens or Water Country USA, depending on how hot it is.

Whitney, Caney Valley KS

Our school is a very small public school (about 80 people per class). We have prom on a Saturday, usually in May. The junior class puts on a banquet and prom for the seniors. They pick ten sophomores to serve and put on skits at the banquet. After the banquet, everyone picks up their dates and comes back to the school. The community shows up to see the dresses, and to see who can show up in the oddest vehicle. We have had people drive racecars, golf carts, hearses, police cars, go-carts and four-wheelers. Inside, the prom king and queen are crowned. After prom, the junior and senior parents hold after-prom, to keep us from getting into trouble. At about four in the morning we leave with our dates and go have breakfast. After breakfast we go to church in our gowns and tuxes.

Lauren, Clarks Summit PA

At my school on the day of prom, we have a triathlon. There are five-person teams as well as people who compete individually. The participants have to run, canoe or swim, and then bike. Each grade has one boys', one girls', and one individuals' race. Then the high school gets out early so everyone can get ready for the prom.

Stephanie, Long Island NY

Hey, it's always been a tradition in my school to go to this island that is on the outskirts of Long Island. Everyone just goes and hangs out on the beach and watches the sunrise. The night before, after prom, everyone usually takes a boat cruise around Manhattan. Very romantic.

Alexia, Mount Sterling KY

At my school, everyone comes to prom in outrageous things. The goal is to do something no one has ever done before. Last year, a couple came via hot air balloon, and another couple came in a helicopter. They have used old cars, Ski-Doos, golf carts, Coke trucks, anything and everything imaginable.

Julie, Gibbsboro NJ

At our school the traditions are that for our sophomore cotillion all the girls should wear a long straight dress, for junior prom we wear ball gowns, and senior prom is fishtail gowns. At cotillion and jr. prom the guys give the girls corsages, but at senior prom it's usually a bouquet or presentation arrangement. After the senior prom the place to be is the shore, where there are usually at least two hotels rented out to our school.

Courtney, Newark DE

I go to an all girls school and we have a partner all boys school. On
the day of prom, the boys go into school in the morning and go to the
auditorium. They have etiquette lessons, including which fork to use,
napkins in the lap, and chew with your mouth closed. Then they proceed to the gym and have a last minute dance lesson (which never
quite teaches them well enough, if you could see their dancing!).
After that, all the guys have to write a letter to their date, and the letter is presented to them at the prom. It's really sweet!

The After-Prom Weekend

After-prom weekends are never sponsored by the school, and rarely organized with any degree of formality. Groups of friends or, occasionally, couples, simply get permission from their parents and either head out to cottages or to beaches, or camping, or any other place where they can have the whole weekend together and just relax and party. After-prom weekend in general is not "traditional" in the sense of all the other traditions printed here. While it is traditional in many areas for seniors (and a very few juniors) to make a weekend of prom night and after-prom—that's why it is part of the master script—there is very rarely a set rule for a given town or school that says "after-prom weekend happens here, or happens this way." In the next story, for example, this couple goes camping for the weekend and it is an individual decision on their part.

Caroline, CT

Well, my prom was pretty cool. I went with this guy I knew, Jared, that I'd been crushing on seriously for like the whole year. I was so petrified to make a fool out of myself, I almost asked somebody I didn't like to go with me! But all I had to do was ask him, because he was going to say yes. If I had known that, it would have saved me a lot of anxiety that he might say no! The dance was so romantic; we danced to almost every song. He kissed me! Anyway, after the prom we all went to the grocery store at around 3 in the morning, to get supplies for a camping trip we were going on for the weekend. Preparing was almost as fun as the prom itself; we danced in the aisles, in our formal wear. The few employees around pumped up the music for us. A piece of advice to everybody: If you want to go with somebody, just ask, it can't hurt. Really. I wasted my whole senior year without making any kind of move, when we could have been together. Oh, and make sure you do something after the prom. Camping was definitely as great as the prom was.

This last story contains another after-prom weekend. I have selected it to wrap up this section because the actual prom night is very close to the master script, from dressing up, to pictures, to the dance itself and then the after-prom. But additionally, it includes an after-prom weekend which, while traditional in that it is part of the master script, is not of itself a well-defined local tradition. As the narrator in this story says, they "went to the beach for the rest of the weekend, but no one else could make it down." In other words, it's not a tradition that everyone in their school who goes to prom also goes to the beach.

When you think about it, there can be no after-prom weekend traditions because there is no institution to get involved in creating and formalizing events into traditions. Ultimately, after-prom weekends are outside the school's—and most parents'—control. You can think of them as the point where prom-goers have at last come of age.

Laurie, Wilmington DE
Well, after a crazy prom date search, I ended up taking the person everyone is convinced I will marry, my best friend, Rich. The family of my other best friend, Lauren, owns a camper...as in a motor home...so we decided that instead of the more traditional limo, we would take that. We all had dates and dresses and transportation! Woo hoo! The day before prom Laur and I and her bf, Nick, got together and washed and decorated the camper. Laur's mom stocked the fridge and even made us chocolate covered strawberries! We had the day of prom all planned out...the girls would meet at my house, and the guys were meeting at Laur's house. They would get the camper and come pick us up...well, Laur's dad was playing chauffeur for the night, but anyway....Well, everything went pretty smoothly...one person was a little late, but we had left a nice window for ourselves, so it was OK. I live in a big historic house, and we have intricate landscaping, so we did pics at my house, and then we were off. The prom was held at a big country club, and it was great! The music rocked, the food was great, pictures were a blast...even the *bathrooms* were nice. Dancing with Rich was a trip...he's a foot taller than me, but I had four inch heels, so it wasn't quite as awkward as jr. prom with him. Afterwards,

there was a parent-sponsored after-prom back at our school, which most people went to. There were games and food and more music…everyone got a door prize and my friend even won a mini-fridge! But the best part of the night was the ride home…snuggled up in Richie's arms in the back of the camper. I didn't want the moment to end. Laur and Nick and Rich and I and another friend, Jen, then went to the beach for the rest of the weekend, but no one else could make it down with us. Prom weekend was the most fun I'd had all year! It was the perfect good-bye!

TYING IT ALL TOGETHER

Definitions and Social Scientists

Every culture sections the passage of time in its own way and then these sections become reality for those who live the culture. In North America we happen to believe there is an entity we call a teenager, and that this entity has clearly defined attributes which make it a "teenager" and not something else. This entity is welded to a particular time and we think of this particular time as a life stage in the overall life cycle—the teen years. We legislate into existence layers of responsibility to differentiate the next life stage—young adulthood—from the teen years, which we then consider to be largely free of responsibility. We attempt to define in general what a teenager is, and what a young adult is, when the transition happens, and how come. We make the end of this life stage coincide with graduation from high school and entry into college or the work force. Finally, we have a party to celebrate the difference between the two, and to celebrate crossing over from one stage into the next.

In the social sciences this definitional process tends to be frowned upon these days as the means whereby those who have power in a culture arbitrarily impose their view of the world on those who don't have power. Social scientists call this "the construction of self," and consider the human body the "site" where this construction happens (they call the body the "contested site," and what is being contested and constructed are "gender," "ethnicity," "teenage," and "young adult" as life stages, etc.). These social scientists say the terms the self uses to construct itself all come from those in power, who supply the "discourses" which then translate into meaning for the constructed individuals. Implied, but usually left unsaid, by these social scientists is the belief that those in power are wrong for doing this, and that they should back off with their terms and discourses so that the self can construct itself in some other way, with a different set of terms and discourses. If you disagree with this, they switch to ad hominem attacks and accuse you of being part of the power structure, insisting that you make yourself willfully blind because you have a strong interest in perpetuating the dominant structure, of translating it into culture. In other words, of making sure your reality gets the best exposure.

Whatever.

The point isn't who supplies your reality. The point is how you live it. It isn't whether teenage years are an artificial construct—obviously they are insofar as all cultural differentiations and distinctions are artificial—the point is that teenage years are experienced as real by those inside the culture and that is what matters.

Going to prom really is a cultural rite. Those who attend senior prom consider it a passage ceremonial, and they believe that the passage takes them from their position as teenage highschoolers to their new position as young adults, with all its attendant rights and responsibilities. Our mainstream culture does not disagree with this, except that it places prom on the teenage side of the passage, which is why we, as adults, can trivialize it. In fact, the silence that comes from the academic community (which has completely ignored prom in its cultural studies) speaks quite loudly to this agreement about what prom is and where it is placed: why research or even discuss something that so obviously belongs to the carefree, irresponsible teenage years when there is important work to be done—you know, the stuff of adulthood, with all its weight-of-the-world urgency?

We have a curious way of ignoring those same "teens" we have apparently "constructed," whether as academic adults conducting teen "discourse" for them—that is, talking about them without consulting them—or as white, largely middle-class, post-industrial whatevers trying to get on with our lives and finding little time for our kids. We just don't seem to think anything teens say or do is particularly important, or that what and how they feel is particularly deep.

And that's too bad.

Because what they feel, what they do and say, is at least as important to them as what we feel, what we do and say is to us.

Tying It All Together

In this book, I have tried to take a truly brief look at how teens feel, at what they do and say, within the context of prom. I write "truly brief" because prom is still more complex than anything I have outlined here; but also, "truly brief" because I cannot have every teen speak in these pages, and I cannot even present every viewpoint teens might share. So I've had to content myself with taking a snapshot, nothing more. Like a snapshot, you capture a little something within the frame, but the great multiplicity of which the snapshot is a tiny extraction keeps right on going all around the lens, the camera, and you. You simply can't catch it all.

I hope I've made the point that prom is not a joke; that it is not frivolous (any more than being a teenager is frivolous); and that it is something fundamentally meaningful not only to the teens who attend it, but to North American culture. I add this last about North American culture because who, after all, makes up our culture if not those who used to be teens? And who will make up tomorrow's culture, if not those who are teens today? Please notice that I use the words "North American culture" and not "popular culture" or "pop culture." Pop culture is typically used by those same social scientists I mentioned earlier, and I get the feeling they use it in an elitist way, as if to say they are not members of popular culture, or that they know better. So I say again, for those who participate in a given culture, even if you call theirs popular culture, bear in mind that this is their culture, and that this is what matters to them. As outsiders, or members of other cultures (whether we define them as ethnic or popular or academic or anything else), we do not have the right to pass judgment on what others find meaningful.

I have said repeatedly in this book that prom has two functions. Both are aspects of the same transition from one life stage to the next. However, one is all about shift in social status as you move out of high school—and that is a graduation. The other is a less sharply defined process which is all about the recognition of one's sexuality and its public confirmation—and that is a coming of age. I don't present these as new and shocking ideas. We all know that prom does this. Most of us have been through either the graduation aspect of it or the coming of age aspect of it, or both. All of us, even those who never attended their own proms (or who are in the few schools that don't have proms), have clearly understood that there is such a thing as a transition from one life stage into the next—we simply haven't used prom to mark it off, that's all. But because the rest of our culture (popular or not) has used it, those of us who missed our proms, or who didn't have one, may have felt a twinge of regret from time to time. At missing prom itself? No, not really. At missing, perhaps, some of what prom has come to represent—because when all is said and done, contemporary prom is like the index to the book containing all the important chapters in our teenage lives.

Peace. Out.

Glossary

Emoticons. Emoticons are used in email and online to convey emotions within the written text. They are always symbols for facial expressions. Here are the ones that appear in this book.

=)	—> Aaaawwwww
:-D or :D	—> Big smile
:-(or :(	—> Sad
:(!)	—> Sad
:-P	—> Tongue hanging out in anticipation
=P	—> Tongue out in anticipation, with squinting smile
;-)	—> Winking; just kidding
:-) or :)	—> Smiling
:o>	—> More smiling

Teen usage. Teens use a few words and phrases somewhat differently these days. Here are the ones that appear in this book and don't seem to be single-instance occurrences.

Bumpin'	—> Said of music; it's good, loud, fast
Crushing	—> Liking someone a lot
Grinding	—> Fast dancing
Hooking up	—> Starting to go out
Hott	—> Very cute
Kewl	—> Cool
Mad-dogged	—> Gave an evil stare
Off the hook	—> Lots of fun, really good

Abbreviations. Writing takes up space, which also means time, and you tend to write in a hurry when it's Internet, often not bothering with spelling or grammar. Abbreviations for common words have evolved to help take up less space, thus cutting down the time you spend writing. These are the main ones that appear in this book.

bf	—> Boyfriend
b/c	—> Because
cuz	—> Because
gf	—> Girlfriend
lol	—> Laugh out loud
msg	—> Message
n	—> And
omg	—> Oh my god
p.o.ed	—> Pissed off
ppl	—> People
r	—> Are
sum1	—> Someone
u	—> You

Emphasis. Sometimes spelling is changed to create emphasis. Here are the ones that appear regularly in this book.

!!, !!!, !!!!	—> Lots of emphasis!!!
ALL CAPS	—> Yelling, or shouting your emphasis
Hella	—> Very
Soo, sooo, sssooo	—> Very, very very
Tonz, tunz	—> A lot of
Woot woot	—> Yeah!

About the Author

Richard Calo received his Ph.D. in comparative literature from
Rutgers, The State University of New Jersey, in 1997. He studies
belief-ritual systems, and focuses on the "true" stories that people use
to convey these systems. He loves collecting the stories people tell
about themselves and their world, and you can often find him chasing
individuals down with a tape recorder or see him locked away in his
office, up to his neck in narratives, blasting Joy Division or Neutral
Milk Hotel as he hunts for what's common in a batch of stories.

In the last six years he has abandoned what he considered the
"straitjacket" of his academic career to do the two things he loves
most: collecting stories and writing about them, and restoring wonderful old houses to their original condition.

His interest in prom as a specific instance of North American
belief-ritual systems arose after he was asked to develop
www.PromDress.Net in 1999 for The Calito Dress Company.

Dr. Calo lives in upstate New York with his wife and three sons.

If you would like to have Richard speak at your school or organiza-
tion, you can contact him at Richard@*The*PromSite.Com.

Notes, Lists, and Stories

These pages are for planning, making notes, and writing your own stories

Notes, Lists, and Stories

These pages are for planning, making notes, and writing your own stories

Notes, Lists, and Stories

These pages are for planning, making notes, and writing your own stories

Notes, Lists, and Stories

These pages are for planning, making notes, and writing your own stories

9 781681 629308